Radcliffe
Biography Series

Dorothy Day

Radcliffe
Biography Series

———

Radcliffe
Biography Series

———

Radcliffe
Biography Series

——

Dorothy Day

A Radical Devotion

——

Robert Coles

A MERLOYD LAWRENCE BOOK

ADDISON-WESLEY PUBLISHING COMPANY, INC.
Reading, Massachusetts   Menlo Park, California
Don Mills, Ontario   Wokingham, England   Amsterdam   Bonn
Sydney   Singapore   Tokyo   Madrid   Bogotá
Santiago   San Juan

Grateful acknowledgment is made to the following for permission to use previously published material:

Harper and Row, Publishers, Inc., for excerpts from *The Long Loneliness: An Autobiography* by Dorothy Day, copyright © 1952 by Harper and Row, Publishers, Inc.

Russell and Volkening, Inc., for an excerpt from *Bread and Wine* by Ignazio Silone, translated by Frances Frenaye, copyright © 1937 by Harper and Row, Publishers, Inc.

Library of Congress Cataloging-in-Publication Data

Coles, Robert.
  Dorothy Day: a radical devotion.

  (Radcliffe biography series)
  "A Merloyd Lawrence book."
  Bibliography: p.
  Includes index.
    1. Day, Dorothy, 1897–1980.   2. Catholics – United
States – Biography.   3. Social reformers – United States –
Biography.   I. Title.   II. Series.
  BX4705.D283C65   1987   267'.182'0924 [B]   87-981
  ISBN 0-201-02829-8

Cover design by Copenhaver Cumpston
Text design by Douglass G. A. Scott
Calligraphy by Jean Evans
Set in 11-point Sabon by Neil W. Kelley, Georgetown, MA

ABCDEFGHIJ–MU–8987

First printing, April 1987

The Radcliffe
Biography Series

Radcliffe College is pleased and proud to sponsor the Radcliffe Biography Series depicting the lives of extraordinary women.

Each volume of the series serves to remind us of two of the values of biographical writing. A fine biography is first of all a work of scholarship, grounded in the virtues of diligent and scrupulous research, judicious evaluation of information, and a fresh vision of the connections between persons, places, and events. Beyond this, fine biographies give us both a glimpse of ourselves and a reflection of the human spirit. Biography illuminates history, inspires by example, and fires the imagination to life's possibilities. Good biography can create lifelong models for us. Reading about other people's experiences encourages us to persist, to face hardship, and to feel less alone. Biography tells us about choice, the power of a personal vision, and the interdependence of human life.

The timeless women whose lives are portrayed in the Radcliffe Biography Series have been teachers, reformers, adventurers, writers, leaders, and scholars. The lives of some of them were hard pressed by poverty, cultural heritage, or physical handicap. Some of the women achieved fame; the victories and defeats of others have been unsung. We can learn from all of them something of ourselves. In sponsoring this series, Radcliffe College is responding to the continuing interest of our society in exploring and understanding the experience of women.

The Radcliffe Biography project found its inspiration in the publication in 1971 of *Notable American Women*, a scholarly encyclopedia sponsored by Radcliffe's Schlesinger Library on the history of women in America. We became convinced that some of the encyclopedia's essays should be expanded into full-length biographies, so that a wider audience could grasp the many contributions women have made to American life – an awareness of which is as yet by no means universal. Since then the concept of the series has expanded to include women of our own times and in other countries. As well as commissioning new biographies, we are also adding reprints of distinguished books already published, with introductions written for the series.

It seems appropriate that an institution dedicated to the higher education of women should sponsor such a project, to hold a mirror up to the lives of particular women, to pay tribute to them, and so to deepen our understanding of them and of ourselves.

We have been joined in this project by a remarkable group of writers. I am grateful to them and to the editorial board – particularly to Deane Lord, who first proposed the series, both in concept and in detail. Finally, I am happy to present this volume in the Radcliffe Biography Series.

Matina S. Horner
President

Radcliffe College
Cambridge, Massachusetts

My wife and I
acknowledge with gratitude and love
the friendship and prayers of Dorothy Day,
their continuing meaning in our lives,
and those of our children.

Contents

Preface

In the spring of 1952, I was a medical student ready to abandon the idea of medicine. On the day that classes ended, I took the downtown subway at Broadway and West 165th Street, hard by the Columbia-Presbyterian Medical Center, where I was going to school. I wasn't quite sure where I was going – only glad to be getting away from where I was. As the train pulled out of the station, a picture of Union Theological Seminary entered my consciousness: that was where I was going. I had been auditing courses there and was especially taken with Reinhold Niebuhr's searching and independent mind. I had also come to know another theologian, David Roberts, who had a strong interest in psychoanalysis but no desire to have it replace the Old and New Testaments as his guiding light. Both of them had mentioned Dorothy Day to me and the fine work being done in Catholic Worker "hospitality houses" all over the country. Their comments had brought back memories of my mother reading the monthly newspaper *The Catholic Worker* in the late 1930s and of my father doing likewise, though with far less enthusiasm.

Those memories again came to mind as I sat in the subway that May morning. Suddenly I realized that classes at Union were probably over, too. I thought of going farther downtown – perhaps to visit the Museum of Modern Art, this time unhurriedly, with no pathology or bacteriology test dominating my conscience. But I was tired of that museum, and of all museums; they reminded me of the very world I yearned to escape, the world of analysis, whether of art or of biology.

I watched the New York City street numbers go by – my mind a blank one moment, all too preoccupied the next, in either case directionless as far as the subway ride was concerned. Finally, as the street numbers got lower and lower, I was forced to make at least one decision: whether to get off in Manhattan or go to Brooklyn, where I had never been. I had just decided to do the latter when I caught sight of an elderly woman and found myself looking at the jaundice in her face, her frail bearing, her swollen ankles. My medical education prodded me – "diagnosis?" As soon as the door opened at the next station, I leaped off and stepped on the escalator, only then smiling at this silly moment of panic, yet another flight from medicine.

I walked and walked, staring at storefronts, people, and cars in their crazy competition. To this day I remember what happened, finally, to stop my aimless wandering. I was standing at a street corner, on Fourteenth Street east of Fifth Avenue, waiting for the lights to change, when I heard someone beside me say "Oh," and again, "Oh." As I turned in the direction of the noise, I saw a woman falling over, onto the cement sidewalk. I reached out by instinct to grab her, to try to interrupt her fall, but I was too late: there she was, on her side, silent. I leaned over, and words automatically left my mouth. "Are you all right?" No answer. "Are you all right?" No answer. As I write these words, I can still feel the tug in me: a desire to leave the scene right away, to keep moving, and a desire to lean over further, to try to talk with the woman, to find out what was wrong, to get some help for her. Several other people were looking at her, but none of us dared get closer or even to touch her, to try to make her feel a bit more comfortable. Finally, after a few seconds, I found myself on my knees, asking the same question, "Are you all right?" She did not answer.

I noticed that her eyes were staring into space, not at me or, apparently, anyone else. I noticed that she didn't seem to be breathing. I became scared. I looked up, saw the face of a man, and shouted for him to try to find a policeman, that the woman lying there was "in bad trouble." He walked into the street of moving traffic, obviously looking for a policeman. As he did so, a man came out of a variety store and told us that he had seen what had happened and had called the police. They arrived in no time, the car pulling up right next to us, the two uniforms descending, and then the decisive look of one of the policemen, which needed no explanation. He shook his head. "She's gone." I thought to myself then, He didn't do a thing—didn't try to take her pulse, didn't try to rouse her. Not that *I* had tried to take a pulse. I had done nothing but ask the same question repeatedly. Otherwise, I had frozen. So had the two or three others who had stayed around. The police made a call, and soon enough the woman, a blanket over her body and her head, was on her way, no longer a cause for alarm or fear or reflection to passersby.

Those of us who had seen her, however, had to come to terms with what we had seen, each in our own way. I kept walking, and for some reason kept remembering not the woman and the scene I had just left, but Union Theological Seminary and what Reinhold Niebuhr and David Roberts had kept reminding their students — that life is brief, that we had best give thought to its overall meaning while we have a chance, before death takes us away.

An hour or so later I showed up at the Catholic Worker soup kitchen on the Lower East Side. I had decided to try to be of help, to do some volunteer work, and remembered hearing of this place. My mind had rumbled along, from thoughts of Niebuhr and Roberts to earlier memories of my Harvard tutor Perry Miller, a professor of English and American literature with a strong interest in the Puritans, their work, and their point of view. This led to memories of the tutoring I had done, as a college student, in what at the time was called a settlement house, where poor children came to be taught, entertained, and fed. At first these memories cast me further adrift. But soon I caught hold of myself and talked to myself: go see if you can find something to do. Another voice, my mother's, reminded me that nothing is worse than aimless discontent or self-pity, which we can cleverly use to show ourselves off as the occasion arises.

xvii

It was on that afternoon, almost thirty-five years ago, that I first met Dorothy Day. She was sitting at a table, talking with a woman who was, I quickly realized, quite drunk, yet determined to carry on a conversation. As I stood nearby, trying to listen in while not appearing to do so, I made a connection between that addled woman and the one I had seen dead on a sidewalk only a few hours earlier. They were approximately the same age and had the same body build (stocky and of medium height) and the same coloring (fair skin, gray-blond hair). The woman to whom Dorothy Day was talking, however, had a large purple-red birthmark along the right side of her forehead. She kept touching it as she uttered one exclamatory remark after another, none of which seemed to get the slightest rise from the person sitting opposite her.

I found myself increasingly confused by what seemed to be an interminable, essentially absurd exchange taking place between the two middle-aged women. When would it end—the alcoholic ranting and the silent nodding, occasionally interrupted by a brief question, which only served, maddeningly, to wind up the already overtalkative one rather than wind her down? Finally, silence fell upon the room. Dorothy Day asked the woman if she would mind an interruption. She got up and came over to me. She said, "Are you waiting to talk with one of us?"

One of us: with those three words she had cut through layers of self-importance, a lifetime of bourgeois privilege, and scraped the hard bone of pride: "Vanity of vanities; all is vanity." With those three words, so quietly and politely spoken, she had indirectly told me what the Catholic Worker Movement is all about and what she herself was like. There would be other lessons, many just as hard to absorb and keep alive within myself. Dorothy Day was a most determined teacher, well aware that in those, like me, who came to learn from her, modesty and humility are poses difficult to sustain for long stretches of time.

I worked as a volunteer at the New York Catholic Worker in the early 1950s while I was in medical school. In the 1960s, when my wife and I went South to study school desegregation and become involved in the civil rights movement, we met Dorothy Day in the region, taking her stand, as she always did, in Mississippi and Louisiana and Alabama. In the early 1970s, by then back in Boston, I wanted to study the history of the Catholic Worker Movement and its connections with other aspects of reform within the church. I began a series of meetings with her; although she was older, she was articulate and vigorous, able to say exactly what she believed, felt, hoped, and feared. By that time I had begun using her books in the courses I teach and bringing my students to Haley House, the Catholic Worker hospitality house in Boston, and to St. Joseph's House and Maryhouse in New York.[1]

In *A Spectacle Unto the World: The Catholic Worker Movement*,[2] I thought I had offered all I could to readers interested in this special "moment" in the Catholic church's continuing life. But in the past five years I have noted that I still get constant inquiries from students, friends, and colleagues about Dorothy Day herself, questions about her attitudes and opinions, her purposes, her hopes and ambitions, the nature of her Christianity, and her politics. The only other figure who, in my experience, elicits a similar urgency of interest is Simone Weil, another twentieth-century religious *and* political woman of a rare sort. My wife and I began asking ourselves the questions others were putting to us with respect to both of those extraordinary women, each drawn to Catholicism as adults rather than born heirs to its traditions and rituals. The result is this book and its spiritual companion, *Simone Weil: A Modern Pilgrimage*.[3]

This is not, strictly speaking, a biography, any more than the Simone Weil book is. The facts of each life are in each book, but what I am trying to do is to examine certain issues and themes that mattered to them – specific aspects of their lives or persisting intellectual interests, beliefs, and obsessions. In the case of Simone Weil, I had to rely on her own notebooks and essays, as well as the comments of her brother and others who knew and had written about her. There is much less biographical writing about Dorothy Day, but she wrote her own substantial autobiography, as well as a number of other books which detail her thoughts about a wide range of subjects. Moreover, for years, every issue of *The Catholic*

Worker contained a column by her, invariably a personal statement as well as an examination of a question that was on her mind at the time. A first-rate biography of her has appeared, and there are several valuable book-length treatments of the Catholic Worker Movement.[4]

I would not be writing this book if I hadn't kept notes for years of conversations I had with Dorothy Day and done repeated tape-recorded interviews with her over a span of two years in the early 1970s.[5] Moreover, she often wrote to me, and when my wife became seriously ill in 1973, she prayed long and hard for her. My wife miraculously – the doctor's word – survived the illness, and she and I have never really been the same since then with respect to our feelings for Dorothy Day, who wrote to us every single morning for a while: a testimony of concern we scarcely know how to acknowledge, even now. God bless her soul.

What I have done, then, is call up the long conversations with her, in the hope of giving readers the benefit of her distinct, compelling point of view. She loved to engage others in talk, and so a large portion of the book follows life: her ideas and words alternating with mine on the topics that always meant so much to her. In the first two chapters and the last one I tend to be relatively more on my own, to introduce her life and try to understand her connection with others whom she loved ardently, but would never presume to link to herself the way someone with the advantage of distance can do.

Before starting I would like to acknowledge again the gratitude to and affection for Dorothy Day that my wife and I feel. I would also like to thank the many students who have kept asking about her life, her beliefs, and her reasons for living as she did. In 1972, I took part in a symposium organized by George Abbott White at the Massachusetts Institute of Technology devoted to the work of Simone Weil. Her brother and I spoke together one afternoon, and I well remember his wry response to the title of the symposium, advertised on billboards, "Simone Weil: Live Like Her?" André Weil turned to me and said, "I doubt many in the audience will want to answer yes to that question." In the case of Dorothy Day, the question is a more plausible one. A few among us may finally be able to say yes. Though I am one who has to answer no, the question has haunted my life. The way people live was of enormous interest to Dorothy Day. She thought hard and long about how one ought to live this life and how one ought to respond to others as they struggle with the same question. Nothing in the following pages is more important, I believe, than her own statements as they pertain to that central matter of moral inquiry: How should we try to live this life?

Dorothy Day

1

——

A Life Remembered

The family background of Dorothy Day was solid, patriotic, and middle class. Her father's family was of Scotch-Irish ancestry, based in Tennessee: they had fought in the Civil War on the Confederate side. Her mother's family was of English ancestry; from upstate New York, they had fought on the Union side. Her parents were married in an Episcopal church on Perry Street in Greenwich Village, where their daughter would spend many years. John Day was a journalist, a racetrack enthusiast, and eventually one of the founders of Hialeah, the first racetrack in Florida. For a time he wrote a column for the New York *Morning Telegraph*, "On and Off the Turf." At the time of his death he was a member of the New York State commission that kept a watch on racetrack activities. Her mother, born Grace Satterlee, cared for the children, encouraged them, and told them what mattered and what did not.

John and Grace Day's third child and first daughter, Dorothy, was born on November 8, 1897, in New York City. Her two older brothers, Donald and Sam Houston, would both become respectable, conservative journalists – Sam, eventually, managing editor of the New York *Journal American*. Dorothy's only sister, Della, to whom she was strongly attached, was two years her junior. The family moved from New York City to San Francisco in 1904, when Dorothy was seven years old. The 1906 San Francisco earthquake destroyed many buildings, among them one where

John Day worked as a sports writer. The Day family soon left for Chicago, where they settled on Chicago's South Side. Because Dorothy's father could not find employment easily, he ended up trying to write a novel, which was never published. In 1907, however, he got a job as the sports editor of *The Inter Ocean*, a Chicago paper, and the family was able to move to the North Side of the city.

When she was sixteen, Dorothy entered the University of Illinois in Urbana, where she would stay only two years. While there she began to call herself a Socialist and to establish friendships with others who, on that midwestern campus, dared pick up the threads of American populism, which had been so influential several decades earlier in the South and the prairie states. At college she was an average student. To supplement her scholarship grant, which she won in a competition supported by the Hearst newspaper the Chicago *Examiner*, she worked at the local Y, changing linen at the dining room tables, and she did household work for professors. At this time she also began to dream of becoming a journalist, a writer. She met a fellow student, Rayna Simons, the daughter of a wealthy Jewish business family. Soon both Dorothy and Rayna became caught up in socialist hopes and concerns. These two students, who became good friends and shared a room, were to live strikingly dramatic and unusual lives. Rayna became a Communist and went to China, then Russia. Her life story – her political and moral pilgrimage – was told in Vincent Sheean's *Personal History*. He desperately wanted to marry her, but she refused him, though she was obviously drawn to him. She died in Moscow of encephalitis in 1927, a little more than a decade after she and Dorothy Day met.

By the time she was nineteen, Dorothy Day had left college and was living in New York, working as a reporter for *The Call*, a socialist paper. Her career as a journalist had started and would continue for the rest of her life. In her early twenties she became very much a part of the radical Greenwich Village scene. Her interest and involvement were based less on theory and ideology than on observation of the world around her and a passionate sense of justice. Her writings were those of a pamphleteer aroused by the poverty and suffering that persisted during America's post–World War I "return to normalcy." She was especially drawn to those who were trying to change the country – labor organizations and people on picket lines. She did not, however, turn her back on the brilliance of the New York intellectual scene. Through her involvement with *The Masses*, she came to know such writers as Mike Gold, Max Eastman, and Floyd Dell, as well as John Dos Passos and Malcolm Cowley. For a while, living on MacDougal Street in Greenwich Village, she seemed to be in continuous conversation – going to lunches and suppers and meetings, waking up with ideas to share with others, and falling asleep with ideas she could barely wait to offer. In 1917, only twenty, she was already in a Washington, D.C., jail, having marched with the suffragettes.

On her return to New York City, she was somewhat aimless. She had left *The Call* and for a while thought she wanted to be a nurse. She took training at Kings County Hospital in Brooklyn for a year but dropped out, unable to sustain the necessary discipline. She worked on the *Liberator*, a radical magazine. She spent a lot of time at the Provincetown Playhouse and had long talks, there and elsewhere, with Eugene O'Neill. They became very close and were known as companions, though the extent of their relationship remains unclear. She also became involved in an unhappy love affair with a tough ex-newspaperman named Lionel Moise, became pregnant by him, had an abortion, and soon thereafter, on the rebound, married Barkeley Tobey, a strange man about whom little is known beyond gossip and the fact that he married eight times. They went to Europe in 1920 and stayed there for a year; Day has made reference to her heavy drinking at that time. When they came back to the States they separated permanently.

Day decided to go to Chicago, where she immediately sought the company of her old midwestern friends, whose populist critique of America's 1920s conservatism had not abated at all. There she went to jail once more, picked up as "dangerous" with her IWW (International Workers of the World, known as "Wobblies") fellow

3

activists during the "red raids" of the period. She spent only a few days in jail, but she would always have a strong memory of that particular experience – the feeling of confinement, of course, but also the degradation of the jailers as well as the jailed. She was touched, too, by the sight of other inmates, the poor, sad people incarcerated for petty crimes and misdemeanors, who, whether they were guilty or not guilty, were clearly headed nowhere. The sentimental side of her, never weak, may well have tried to ignore the specific wrongdoings of those people. Her account of her stay in jail dwells mainly on the prostitutes with whom she shared a cell, particularly their stubborn determination and their generosity and kindness to her.

She would often hark back to that prison stay in the conversations I had with her. Once she told me that "the experience of being in jail *then* [after the turmoil she had been through in her emotional life] had a strong impact" on her way of looking at the world. She came to prison a Wobbly in spirit, full of egalitarian dreams for America. She left prison in a less romantic frame of mind with concrete memories of women who could be called streetwalkers, prostitutes, whores, and names that would call attention to their law-breaking lives, but whose fate kept pushing her to moral reflection. She was, by that time, quite ready to accept the paradox of kindly, sensitive women who helped her get through the days in prison yet could go back on the street to sell themselves, perhaps to steal, and be cruelly indifferent to others in the course of their everyday lives.

Often, as I talked with her, I felt her discomfort with certain memories – discomfort, really, with her earlier life and her "bohemian" past. She seemed uncomfortable even with the aspects of her past which persisted as strengths in her later life: the writer, the political activist, the woman prepared to break ranks with society's norms in order to uphold moral principles. Several times she told me that her "life really did begin" when she "met Peter [Maurin]," and she grew annoyed when I demurred. Yet the continuities in her life are striking; in her "fast" life of the early 1920s and the life that followed her conversion to Catholicism, the same awareness and ideals can be found.

4

For example, when she thought back to the Wobbly incident and her jailing, she would talk of a particular inmate Mary-Ann, who was especially considerate and made that stay behind bars much more bearable. A woman who had little education, she was "a woman of the streets," but also a teacher, not unlike Peter Maurin, both in her message, as Dorothy Day recalled it, and in her influence on the person whose life supposedly "began" only years later.

"I can still hear Mary-Ann giving me my lessons in survival – how to get along with the people running the prison," she once told me. Then she spelled out Mary-Ann's teaching – a mix of ethical exhortation and practicality: "'You must hold up your head high, and give them no clue that you're afraid of them or ready to beg them for anything, any favors whatsoever. But you must see them for what they are – never forget that they're in jail, too.'" A pause, then: "Many times, so many times, I remember that admonition. Mary-Ann had no use for organized religion. She had never finished high school, but in her head and her heart she had somehow drawn near our Lord. Nearer than I was able to get, then. Who knows, nearer than some of us ever get."

During that prison stay Dorothy Day read the Bible, taking particular comfort in the Psalms. But she was not yet tempted by "organized religion." In Chicago she continued her journalistic endeavors and investigated the way the courts treated juveniles and prostitutes. Ben Hecht and Charles MacArthur, who were her friends, were doing similar muckraking. She also worked a while as a clerk in a library, a proofreader, a restaurant cashier, and a clerk in a Montgomery Ward's. She even posed for art classes. The word *drifting* has been applied to this time of her life.[1] Yet one gathers from listening to her that while going from job to job to eke out a living, she was trying to learn how all sorts of people spend their working lives. She wasn't simply "slumming." She had been on her own since she left home for college at seventeen. Her father and older brothers had never approved of her manner of living, her political sympathies, or her activism. Moreover, in the 1920s it was not easy for a woman, especially one who was thoughtful about social and economic matters and critical of America's politics, to find a decent job. For a while she tried New Orleans, where she worked with the *Item*, lived in the French Quarter, and, as a journalist, returned to her interest in exploited women. "I wrote articles on dance-hall girls," she once put it, and yet again, as she talked about them, one could hear her empathy for what such women experience and a willingness – perhaps in the tradition of her friend "Gene" O'Neill – to see them as judges of the rest of us, rather than as morally flawed or suspect.

While in Chicago she had written an autobiographical novel, *The Eleventh Virgin*. Years later she would regret ever having published it and wished that every extant copy could through some magic be destroyed. In New Orleans she learned that Hollywood had bought the book for $5,000, a substantial sum at the time. The novel is candid about the young heroine – her lusty and unconventional life, her brief and tragic romance, her abortion, her loveless marriage, and her constant traveling. The wretched plot is lightened by the narrator's sense of humor and her capacity to observe ordinary people, the strangers we all see but tend not to notice. Whether she was in jail, simply walking in the street, buying groceries, asking directions, browsing in a bookstore, or waiting in line to enter a theater or a museum, Dorothy Day was constantly noticing people, constantly ready to engage with them and let them become, even for a few moments, part of her life. This unusual quality, which I watched at work in her, would not yield even to old age, a time when so many of us are inclined to put more and more barriers between ourselves and others, often impelled to do so by nature itself: the way aging can isolate us, restricting both our mental and physical capacities.

With the money from her book she was able to leave New Orleans, return to New York, find a cottage on the beach in Staten Island, and pursue the career of a serious writer. At twenty-eight, she was anxious to settle down, to test decisively her literary ability, and, for the first time, to build a home for herself. She lived in the Staten Island cottage for four years. In retrospect, one evening late in her life, when she was seventy-two, she connected her literary ambition with the sea.[2]

"I was born within sight of the Brooklyn Bridge, and I remember my mother telling us how much she enjoyed the sight of the Pacific Ocean. I also remember how much she enjoyed walking along the shore of Lake Michigan, and I can hear her now saying that she could never live in a city where there is no water nearby. Bread and water – what Christ knew we all need. For me water is a reminder of Him. But I didn't have such thoughts when I was in my twenties. As I look back, I can remember how often I would seek the water in New York City, in Chicago, in New Orleans. All the days and months blur, but not the sight in my mind of Lake Michigan and the Atlantic Ocean and the Hudson River and the East River and the Mississippi River and the Potomac River – the comfort of seeing water. Even when I was in Washington for a few days, to picket and march, I wanted to see the river. No wonder I started to write near the ocean."

These thoughts seemed to make her feel at once detached from her past and amused by it. As I pressed her for details about that period in her life, however, she became cranky, impatient, and returned to the image of "water" coming up yet again.

"You're asking me for dates and for the names of people, and that's not what matters. If you want to think of me in my twenties, think of someone drifting – I won't deny it – but drifting on water. I hadn't asked *whose* water until I was in my late twenties, not seriously; but I do recall looking at the driftwood I'd see along the Staten Island shore and thinking of myself. Being near the ocean gave me strength to go through the motions of living, even when I was feeling lost and alone during difficult times."

By 1925 she was in love again, with a man who, although he was more stable and worthy of her than her former lovers, would in his own way cause her "difficult times." Forster, as she referred to him in her writing and in conversations (his last name was

7

Batterham) was a biologist, an anarchist, and not least, an atheist. Theirs was "a common-law marriage," she said in *The Long Loneliness*. She had been introduced to him by his sister Lily, who was the writer Kenneth Burke's first wife. Born in North Carolina, Batterham had a radical, agrarian sensibility: their politics were compatible. For several years they were happy together, but she then wanted a child. He was gloomy about the world's prospects and had no interest in seeing, through his own offspring, another generation struggle to make things better. When Sacco and Vanzetti were sent to the electric chair, he was devastated, went into a deep depression, and was convinced that what had happened to them was a definitive statement of how people behave toward one another. In Dorothy Day's words, admittedly spoken from a half century's distance, "The execution of those two men, who were such fighters for the poor and who were so eloquent – for Forster it was as if all the decency in the world had been killed with them."

By then, however, Forster had become a parent. Their daughter, Tamar Teresa, was born in March 1927. Before her birth they had been very much a part of New York's radical and literary world. So many of their friends now are recognized as "famous," but at the time they were, like Dorothy Day herself, struggling hard to become novelists or poets, to change the world through polemical writing or political action: Hart Crane, Allen Tate, Caroline Gordon, and of course, Malcolm Cowley, John Dos Passos, Eugene O'Neill, Mike Gold, and Kenneth Burke. All those names, and others, appear in *The Long Loneliness*. A few years away from her death, Dorothy Day would look back at her words, her mention of these friendships, with unflinching self-scrutiny.[3]

"We were all friends, and we shared a lot of our hopes and our troubles with each other. When I read some of my words, though [in *The Long Loneliness*], or when the young people start asking me about those days, and all the 'people' I knew, I feel uncomfortable; I feel as if I've been a terrible name-dropper. I once asked a priest to forgive me for name-dropping. He asked what I meant. I told him. He laughed, and he said it

8

sounded to him as if I was just remembering some old friends of mine. I *was* doing that, yes; but there were other friends, and I didn't mention them. When I told the priest that, he wasn't too impressed. He said I'm a writer and I was 'sharing' something with my readers. Yes, I answered, but two words just came out of me before I knew what was happening, and suddenly I heard them, to my surprise and shame: 'my pride!'"

Tamar Teresa was born eight months before her mother's thirtieth birthday. Dorothy Day wrote a much admired article describing the birth of her baby for *New Masses*; she was as happy as she had ever been. On the other hand, Forster was far from exultant. A thoroughly decent man, he still loved Dorothy and was not about to turn his back on their daughter. Yet he soon began to realize that it was not only parenthood to which he had to accommodate himself. First, his daughter was baptized in the Catholic church in July of 1927, when she was a few months old; then Dorothy Day became increasingly interested in that church herself. She and Forster separated for good in late December, when she asked to be baptized in the Catholic church. "I think I realized on the day I was baptized," she once said, "how long I had been waiting for that moment — all my life." In fact, she believed her life had just begun, though many of her friends thought quite the contrary.

In any case, she was going to live differently for the remaining fifty-three years of her life. She left Staten Island with her infant daughter and moved into an apartment on West Fourteenth Street "in order to be near Our Lady of Guadalupe Church." Always a reader of novels and social or political essays, she now read philosophy and theology as well. She had found a confessor, Father Zachary, and she turned to him almost daily. She was not only a Catholic, but a Catholic who wanted to learn how to live her life according to the teachings of Jesus Christ, whom the church claims as its founder. Put differently, her conversion was not nominal.

In the months and years that followed, however, Dorothy Day continued to wonder what she ought to be doing, how she ought to spend the time she had been given on this earth. She still went to the theater often and was especially taken with the performances of Eva Le Gallienne's troupe. She kept seeing her old friends. Still the social activist, concerned about the poor, and worried about the hate in this world between races and nations, she got a job working with the Fellowship of Reconciliation. She wrote a play that elicited the interest of a number of New York directors and producers and, eventually, some Hollywood people. Though it was never produced, she was given a contract with Pathé and went to Hollywood, where she worked as a filmwriter for a while. It was not a world she could stomach, however, and she soon left for Mexico, staying with a friend in Mexico City for several months. She liked living in Mexico – the warmth, the casual but omnipresent Catholicism. But Tamar fell sick, and they hurried back to New York.

It was the time of the Great Depression, and she could not ignore what she saw around her everywhere – the widespread poverty and pain of men and women who walked the streets hoping for a job, a handout, anything. As she watched so many people endure humiliation and jeopardy, she began to wonder why the major institutions of the nation were unwilling, she believed, to respond to the need for food, shelter, and clothing. America was a rich and powerful nation, and in New York, as well as in other American cities, she had seen how much wealth was available: blocks and blocks of fancy townhouses and apartment houses and stores and churches, including Catholic ones, to which came flocks of well-dressed, well-fed parishioners. She could not simply accept the disparities of "the facts of life." She read the Bible and went to church every day; she read papal encyclicals or books devoted to Catholic social teaching, and she felt that Christ's words, His example, and His admonitions had somehow been forgotten, even by priests and nuns, bishops and cardinals.

Her response was not to turn on the church, but rather to pray for it, as she prayed for her friends and for herself. Moreover, she was only too aware of her own confusions and the mistakes she had made in her personal life. She worried that her moral outrage would consume her, turning her into a bitter or smugly self-righteous person:[4]

"I remember those days, before I met Peter Maurin: I was on the brink of losing my faith, having just become a Catholic. I was very upset by what I saw – the church's apparent indifference to so much suffering. In [the early years of the Depression] people walked the streets, hundreds and hundreds of them, looking dazed and bewildered. They had no work. They had no place to go. Some groups tried to help them, but neither the state nor the church seemed as alarmed as my 'radical' friends."

In *The Long Loneliness*, speaking of those friends and their activities on behalf of the poor, she made this observation: "There was Catholic membership in all these groups, of course, but no Catholic leadership. It was that very year [1929] that Pope Pius XI said sadly to Canon Cardijn, who was organizing workers in Belgium, 'The workers of the world are lost to the Church.'"[5]

She would never forget that papal statement. It can be said that her entire life from 1932 until her death was dedicated to working against its assumptions. It was in November of 1932 that she learned of a "hunger march" to Washington, an effort to make known loudly and clearly to the nation's leaders what was happening to millions of its citizens. She had, by then, written many pieces for *Commonweal*, a liberal Catholic magazine, and she wanted very much to record what happened to the hundreds who assembled in Union Square, her old political haunt, in order to take their cause to the steps of America's Capitol Building. She was working on a second novel, one she called a social novel, a story meant to convey the everyday experiences of down-and-out, jobless people. Her trip to Washington would interrupt that writing, but she was glad for such an interruption.

While in Washington, on December 8, 1932, saddened and angered by what she saw in Union Square, on the way to Washington, and in that city – a small army of desperately impoverished and vulnerable people who were pleading for food, for a chance to work, to assert their dignity as citizens – she went to the National Shrine of the Immaculate Conception at Catholic University and prayed with all her heart and soul for a chance to "use what talents" she could find within herself for her "fellow workers, for the poor." On her return to New York City she found a man named Peter Maurin waiting for her. George M. Shuster, then *Commonweal*'s editor, had come to know Maurin, and of course had admired his contributor Dorothy Day for some time. He recognized their similarity of views and shared willingness to mix religion and politics as activists. Maurin was quick to accept Shuster's suggestion that he meet Dorothy Day, talk with her, and determine with her what might be done on behalf of the poor.

For days that became weeks and then months, the two of them talked, trying to figure out what each might do to change the dismal contemporary American scene for the better. Gradually Dorothy got to know Peter, learning enough about him to realize what an extraordinary person he was and how congenially he and she were able to work together. She learned, too, about his earlier life: a childhood in a large, rural, French Catholic family; his membership in the Saint Jean-Baptiste de La Salle brotherhood, a group of men who never became priests but taught the children of the poor and shunned honors and privileges, even within the church. He took his first annual vows in 1895 and learned to be a teacher. He was sent to Paris, where he eventually became involved in the Sillon Movement, a reformist Catholic effort at spiritual renewal much influenced by the May 15, 1891, landmark encyclical *Rerum Novarum* of Pope Leo XIII, in which he called for social justice – for the rich and powerful to share more of what they had with the needy. Maurin took the pacifism of the Sillon Movement – the pacifism of the message Jesus offered his followers – seriously enough to leave France rather than submit to the required military service. In 1909 he went to Canada. He had, by then, been much influenced by Pyotr Kropotkin's *Fields, Factories and Workshops* and *Mutual Aid*, with their stress on the spiritually redemptive value of community farms and small home crafts. Kropotkin saw the people of his time as too removed from any satisfying sense of personal usefulness. Maurin had a vision of small communities in which families once again produced food, clothes, and houses, regaining control over the day-to-day substance of their lives – no doubt a utopian vision, as was Kropotkin's and that of Tolstoy, who also became a strong influence on the young French exile.

Once in Canada he headed for the wheat fields of Alberta, where he had hoped to homestead with a friend. But the friend was killed in an accident, and Maurin became a wanderer, digging ditches, harvesting crops, quarrying stone, doing construction work, working in a coal mine, riding the freight trains, and taking jobs in factories. By 1925 he had worked his way to New York, and for several years thereafter spent his time reading in the public library – books on moral philosophy, religion, sociology, and economics. He also started writing his "Easy Essays" – brief, strong pieces, each of which attempted to state the nature of a particular social problem, then to suggest a direct, practical response to it that would be in the spirit of the teachings of Jesus. By the time he and Dorothy Day met, those essays had become an art form all their own. Each had a distinctive message delivered in short sentences, sometimes repeated for emphasis, though the repetitions were also amplifications; Maurin arranged the sentences in verse form, a few words or a phrase on one line, the end of the sentence on the next, employing rhyme sometimes or pointed similes and metaphors.

On many occasions Dorothy made it quite clear that for her Peter's "spirit and ideas" were utterly essential to the rest of her life. She was inspired by his struggle to make the principles of Jesus incarnate in the kind of life he lived, to rescue them from those who had turned Him into an icon of Sunday convenience. The Catholic Worker Movement became their shared initiative.

The newspaper came first, of course: they were both writers. On May Day 1933 the two of them had 2,500 copies of *The Catholic Worker* available for distribution. They had not opened an office, hired a staff, secured mailing lists, or planned elaborate promotion. They had raised $57 from two priests and a nun and from their own almost empty pockets, and with the help of a printer had put out what Dorothy Day would later describe as a "small eight-page sheet the size of *The Nation*." Then came the attempt to attract readers, by a long march from the Lower East Side to Union Square, where they joined the political crowds assembled there and peddled their paper, no doubt to the surprise of many onlookers, for whom the juxtaposition of "Catholic" and "worker" seemed anomalous.

In a way, as Dorothy Day herself once put it, "the rest was history." She was not being grandiose, as she made clear by her immediate qualifications. "I mean by 'history' the history of all of us who have been part of the Catholic Worker family. That's what happened, that's what we became, a family spread across all the cities and states of this country." Within a few years, *The Catholic Worker* had a circulation of over a hundred and fifty thousand, with many more readers than that figure suggests, because it has always been a paper that is handed from person to person. It is a monthly which, to this day, sells for "a penny a copy."

Yet Dorothy Day and Peter Maurin were not content simply to write about what they believed the Catholic church has to offer the ordinary worker, to publish their moral and political philosophy. They both believed in the importance of "works." Together they founded the hospitality houses that became part of the American social scene for men and women who had no other place to go, nothing to eat, and were at the mercy of whatever secular or religious charity happened to be available. Peter Maurin envisioned a twentieth-century version of the ancient notion of a hospice, a place where "works of mercy" were offered and acknowledged in a person-to-person fashion, as opposed to the faceless, bureaucratic procedures of the welfare state. He shared that vision with Dorothy Day. Together they started to make that vision real, by renting a store, an apartment, buying bread and butter, making coffee, preparing soup, serving food to the homeless, finding clothes for them, offering them, when possible, a place to sleep, and very important, sitting with them, trying to converse, hoping in some way to offer them friendship and affection. Other people joined to help, and in time there would be over thirty "houses of hospitality" across the nation. Over the years more have started, folded, and sometimes got going again.

The Catholic Worker has dwelt often on the moral as well as political significance of agriculture. Beyond its obvious purpose of growing food, it is also an antidote to the alienation caused by industrialism, which separates us from the bare bones of life and makes us spend entire lives in offices or on assembly lines. Farms were built up by the men and women and children who became part of the Catholic Worker family in New England and New York State, in Appalachia, in the Midwest, and on the Pacific Coast. In all those places knots of kindred souls became centers of action. Newspapers appeared in Chicago, Buffalo, St. Louis, Seattle, Houston, Los Angeles, and as far away as England and Australia. There was no party line, no set of rules or positions handed down to the various hospitality houses or farms or newspapers. Thousands of men and women the world over responded in various ways to the example and determination of two Catholic laypersons, Dorothy Day and Peter Maurin.

From May Day 1933 until November 29, 1980, when she died, Dorothy Day lived without interruption as a Catholic Worker. She edited the paper of that name, she lived in the hospitality houses of that name, and she traveled by bus across the United States, teaching and speaking, helping to cook, and sitting with people the rest of us call bums or homeless or drunks. She also kept saying her prayers, going through devotional rhythms, reading and rereading the books she loved, and writing her *Catholic Worker* column, "On Pilgrimage." Tamar grew up at her side, then left, married, and made her mother a grandmother numerous times.

During those years Dorothy Day took on many a controversy. She stood up to Franco when he started the Spanish civil war, thereby losing lots of Catholic readers who saw Franco as a godsend who was leading a Catholic charge against the atheists, the Communists who had taken over Spain. She argued the case for pacifism during the Second World War, a lonely stance, indeed, and one that many of her closest friends, her most enthusiastic coworkers adamantly rejected. After the war, she continued her work among the poor and on behalf of those whom we now call minorities. (One of the first efforts she and Peter Maurin made was in Harlem, at the very start of their work together.) I well remember her, during the 1960s,[6] riding buses in the South, involving herself in the civil rights struggle, and showing up on the West Coast alongside Cesar Chavez. By then she was a veteran of marches and demonstrations and picket lines and jails, someone who had learned to live simply, travel lightly. Wherever she was, she found time every day for prayer, for reading the Bible, for attending Mass, taking Communion, and saying confession.

The last time I saw her, not long before her death, I had taken a group of my students to the Catholic Worker office, to St. Joseph's House, and to Maryhouse, where she lived.[7] She was frail, but she stood straight and was as gracious as she had been years earlier, when she had the strength to serve personally the hundreds of homeless people who came daily to the Catholic Worker kitchen for soup and coffee and bread. We shared a few memories, and I asked her what she was reading and whether she was doing any writing. She was reading, yet again, her beloved Tolstoy – "The Death of Ivan Ilyich" – and Dickens – *Little Dorrit*. Her eyes were full of life, no matter the diminished capacity of her lungs, the compromised exertions of her heart muscles. "It will soon be over," she told me, then added,

> "I try to think back; I try to remember this life that the Lord gave me; the other day I wrote down the words 'a life remem-bered,' and I was going to try to make a summary for myself, write what mattered most – but I couldn't do it. I just sat there and thought of our Lord, and His visit to us all those centuries ago, and I said to myself that my great luck was to have had Him on my mind for so long in my life!"

I heard the catch in her voice as she spoke, and soon her eyes were a little moist, but she quickly started talking of her great love for Tolstoy, as if, thereby, she had changed the subject.

An Inquiring Idealism

Over the past half century many young men and women have been drawn toward the Catholic Worker Movement, considering its principles and approach to social problems compelling enough to warrant serious study or a commitment of time and energy. By no means have all of them been professing Catholics or Christian or even religious in any conventional or explicit sense of the word. Agnostics and atheists in significant numbers have found their way to the hospitality houses and devoted time to them.[1]

The hospitality houses are places where one can do concrete work on behalf of others. Many young men and women who feel within themselves surges of idealism don't know what to do about it. A skeptic might say that they don't look hard enough, but it isn't always easy for people to find opportunities for charity in the biblical sense of the word, free of the implication of condescension. In the hospitality houses there is an immediacy to the charitable gesture, a directness, unmediated by bureaucracy and self-consciousness, that many young people find appealing.

The intellectual side of the Catholic Worker tradition, with its interest in ethical inquiry, is also of interest to students and others who are trying hard to connect the work of philosophers and novelists and historians to their own lives. Peter Maurin was himself part of an idealistic youth movement that inspired many hundreds of French men and women.[2] Dorothy Day began her social activism

on the campus of the University of Illinois and for years was willing
to go talk with young people, wherever and whenever they invited
her to come, within the limits of her own obligations.

She never ceased being interested in young people, responsive
to their questions, and aware of their hungers and thirsts. Nor did
she allow her own hard-won faith to come between herself and
others. This openness to the doubts of others must have required
effort on her part, or so I often thought as I talked with her, feeling
the intensity of her faith in her every breath. One afternoon, as
she was remembering her time as a college student and as a young
woman living in Manhattan, full of literary aspirations and political
ideas, we drifted gradually into a more general discussion of
idealism and its nature, possibilities, and dangers.[3] "When young
people come here," she said,

"we are grateful for their interest. I have watched some of them,
trying so hard to talk with those men and women standing in line
or sitting with their coffee and soup. The students know so much,
and yet they are learning. The poor who come here feel there is
little they have to offer anyone, and yet they have a lot to offer.
The giving and the receiving is not only going on in one direction.

"When I left home and came to Urbana it was as if I'd been
shown the Promised Land. I wasn't happy all the time there, but I
was free, 'free at last.' I have heard Dr. King speak, and I have
thought to myself that many of the white young people who have
become so involved with the civil rights movement have known a
little of what the Negro people – the black people, we're to say
now – have known. I don't mean personal unhappiness, no; I'm
not saying that family turmoil leads young people to social action, heavens no. Maybe sometimes – but I'm sure you know
plenty of young people who come from quite troubled homes,
and they certainly don't become involved with Dr. King's SCLC
or with Catholic Worker people."

She was, I believe, referring to the awareness of injustice or
inequality or unfairness that so many children, no matter how

fortunate their circumstances, manage to develop and, to some extent, hold in their consciousness. Many youths in the civil rights movement told me of the connections they made between racial bias and apparently "minor" everyday incidents – a parent or teacher "playing favorites," for instance. They gradually become aware that racial prejudice has similar origins: that a nation can be similarly prejudiced or ill-disposed toward some of its people.

"I think it is natural for young people to try to look a little beyond themselves," she went on,

"more so than most older people. So many men and women become *bound* – they have all they can do to take a deep breath and fall asleep at night. They've been on the go from dawn, and they're hounded by the everyday burdens of just keeping even with things. It's very hard to tell intellectuals that, to get them to look at the life most workers live. Peter used to tell me, over and over, that college professors and college students are living in 'a very special world.' (He was always polite and respectful.) He reminded me that the same holds for writers, for journalists. We're not 'pushed,' you might say, the way workers are. We have more freedom. We can let loose with our ideas – we're paid to do that. Yes, true, we have to make a living, also, I agree. But it's not quite the same. We don't work so directly for a factory time clock, and we have a little more flexibility in our lives, breathing space.

"When I was in college, and when I lived in New York, there was something in me – long before I met Peter – that made me stop and look at people, at certain people, and wonder and wonder about their lives, how they lived, and wonder if I could ever do it, live the way they did. I had to work fairly hard myself as a student; I had no pot of gold to draw from, no sir. The expression years ago was 'shake a leg'; I had to shake a leg if I was going to stay in school, and when I left and lived in New York and then Chicago, I was always needing a job or having to find some way to keep ahead. But no matter what I did or where I was, I'd end up, most any day, picking someone to stare at. I would wonder how in the world the person got through each day. Idealism in the young, I guess I'm saying, is curiosity as well as goodness trying to express itself. And it's knowledge of your own pain, which you see in your neighbor. But there's nothing new in saying that."

Despite her modest demurrer, I thought her choice of the word *curiosity* an interesting one – not an attribute usually discussed in connection with idealism.[4] Her own idealism was evident well before she left home for college, an idealism both precocious and prophetic and connected in her mind with wanderlust, with a desire to see the world, to read eagerly, constantly. In a letter written in 1912, when she was only fifteen, and quoted at length in *The Long Loneliness*,[5] she comes across as not unlike the Dorothy Day the world had come to know by the time the autobiography was published in 1952. She quotes from Tennyson; she makes reference to reading Dostoievski; she refers repeatedly to God ("Every day belongs to God and every day we are to serve Him doing His pleasure"), though she already knows that "only after a hard bitter struggle with sin, and only after we have overcome it, do we experience blessed joy and peace."

In the autobiography, she immediately turns on her young self from the distance of her middle-aged life. "Written when I was fifteen, this letter was filled with pomp and vanity and piety. I was writing of what interested me most, the conflict of flesh and spirit, but I was writing self-consciously and trying to pretend to myself I was being literary." She *was* being literary, and successfully. She was also busy with the world, investigating it through her feverish reading, making connections between the literary imagery and what she could find in the world.

When I read *The Jungle* by Upton Sinclair, I began taking long walks toward the West Side rather than going to the park or lake [in Chicago]. I walked for miles, pushing my brother in his carriage, often with my sister at my side, she usually holding on to the carriage, too. We explored until we were footsore, going up and down interminable gray streets, fascinating in their sameness, past tavern after tavern, where I envisaged such scenes as that of the Polish wedding party in Sinclair's story, past houses which were sunk down a whole story below street level for block after block.

For Dorothy Day the connection between "art" and "life" was real, substantial, a powerful influence on her everyday actions. Idealism is, after all, literally a pursuit of the ideal, usually in one's head, sometimes with one's whole body. Well before she had become a college Socialist or a New York bohemian politically engaged with radical groups or a Catholic convert ready to give her life for the welfare of others, Dorothy Day was busy searching out one book's moral message, then another's, and trying to determine whether her own life passed muster. Dostoievski would not let her sleep. Tennyson stirred her to romantic anguish. Passages from the Bible's words somehow stood out, as if meant for her. "I know it seems foolish to try to be so Christ-like, but God says we can. Why else His command, 'Be ye therefore perfect.'"

Even then she was the moral explorer whose intense curiosity about life was excited both by what she read and what she saw. Books fed her passion to witness and experience more of the world. Her reminiscences reminded me of some of the secular idealists I met during the civil rights activism of the early 1960s and the literary side of their idealism. As we talked about their lives, their purposes, they kept mentioning *Invisible Man, Let Us Now Praise Famous Men, Light in August, The Sound and the Fury*, and stories by Richard Wright or by Chekhov or Tolstoy. At times they made a point of putting that literature aside, emphasizing the reality of, say, the Delta and its segregationist power or Alabama and its unyielding resistance to change, as if a literary reference would seem self-indulgent and callous against such commonplace, harsh racial and social realities. Yet, as I listened to particular young men and women in those days, the influence of literature in their lives repeatedly became apparent.[6]

Once I shared with Dorothy Day some tapes of interviews I had done during the Mississippi Summer Project, when some five hundred American college students – many of upper-middle-class white background – spent several months trying to help black people register to vote. As we sat and listened to those voices, she was prompted to comment on her own Southern experience. A bit later, we listened again, not so much for the political content – the stories they had told about the experiences in the civil rights movement – as for the moral tone of their remarks. She was interested in what had made these particular youths embark on such a course of action. Religious values? Secular values? Noblesse oblige? A spirit of adventure? All of those, and maybe any number of idiosyncratic motives?

These questions made her think back to her own life, and she was hard put to single out the source of her youthful moral energy. Her parents, she told me, were not particularly interested in social issues. She has written that her father, of Southern ancestry, had "the prevalent attitude of the South toward the Negro." She added that "he distrusted 'foreigners' and 'agitators,'" including the radical movement which she and her sister joined. Her mother's horizons were domestic. "Whenever mother had extra troubles or a specially hard day's work behind her, she used to bathe and dress with particular care as though she were giving a dinner party. She reigned over the supper table as a queen and had as much interest in entertaining her four children as if we were all adult friends in for a party." Except for these festive meals, one gathers, the children were left to fend for themselves and not encouraged to think about the outside world. "There were times when my sister and I turned to housework from sheer boredom!"[7]

As Dorothy Day listened to those tapes and remembered her earlier years, she began to ask herself, as she had when she wrote *The Long Loneliness*, how it had all come about.[8]

"I don't know what events made me become the person I am. People have asked me, and I retire in silent ignorance. When I wrote *The Long Loneliness* I wanted to confess – tell people that I'd been a seeker as a young woman, but had struggled with my instincts, the way you people [psychiatrists] say we do.

[She had written in that book that "the world meant the flesh and the lure of the flesh, the pride of life one felt when in love." She then added, "This conflict was to go on for years."] But when I listen to those tapes, I realize that it's not idealism *as against* sensuality, or self-sacrifice *as against* self-centeredness; and it's not idealism as the result of a child's home life, or in reaction to it; it's idealism as a drive itself, as one of those instincts people say are so fundamental."

She paused, and I was glad, because I wasn't quite sure I would be able to follow her unless we both stopped and tried to figure out what she meant. Her explanation went like this:

"As far back as I can remember I asked questions about 'life' — why we're here and where we're going. I have read Freud, many of his books, and books by other psychoanalysts, and I know that children are curious about sex, and that curiosity makes them inquisitive in general, as must have been the case with Freud himself. But sometimes I wonder which is the cart and which is the horse. Perhaps I'm trying to forgive myself for some of my sins, but there are times when I sit here and sip coffee and stare out that window and watch people hurrying along, and I think back and remember myself, hurrying along from meeting to meeting and party to party, and all the friends and the drinking and the talk and the crushes and falling in love and the disappointments and the moments of joy — it all seems part of the seeking and questioning I used to do when I'd be exploring the streets or going to church and wondering what those ministers were like and why they became ministers and whether that meant they were any better than my father or any of the other grown-up men I knew. Once I asked my father why people become what they become — did what they did. He said he didn't know. I thought the subject was over, for good. He was one person we never nagged. But a couple of days later, we were eating supper, and he told me that he was still thinking about 'that question' I had asked him, and he hadn't come up with any answer, but he had a thought.

"Well, I had almost forgotten the question – not quite, though. I was so proud, I remember, to have said something that stuck in his mind. I think my mother was surprised. I think she felt that he hadn't always given us as much attention as he might have, though he was very busy and hard-working. I waited for my father to tell me what he was thinking, but he didn't say anything, so I asked. I can hear his answer, right now in my mind. My father said, 'Most people fall into what they do by luck, good luck and bad luck, but not wholly, because even the poorest person can choose among all the very tough jobs, so the answer is that we're born with a temperament, and it's our temperament that pushes us to do the work we do.' That was his message, and of course I wanted to know what 'temperament' means. I still do. I think he was trying to say that some of us are good at doing certain things and good at asking certain questions and good at trying to find the answers to them, and other people have other questions on their mind. I know someone who is an electrical engineer, and when I talk with him I realize that all his life he's been asking an electrical engineer's questions. That's what he told me once!

"When we become grown up, I'm saying, all the sexual energy Freud has told us about pushes us to inquire even more, to seek not only love – a man for a woman, a woman for a man – but answers to our questions. Your profession calls it sublimation, but I think ideas like sublimation don't explain all of our curiosity. I mean, we're born to ask questions and to come up with answers, and so we look to God, and we look to sublimation to explain things, and we have faith in both. But for me faith is not diminished by this kind of talk. God put us here to go through this kind of mental gymnastics, and He certainly put us here to enjoy our sexual lives. He put us here to *ask*, to try to find out the best way possible to live with our neighbors. Of course, you can go through a life not asking, and that's the tragedy: so many lives lived in moral blindness."

All her life she struggled also with another kind of "conflict" than the lure of the flesh mentioned in *The Long Loneliness*. I remember a long conversation in March 1970.[9] It was bitterly cold and windy outside, as the afternoon sun gradually dimmed. She was thinking back on the years of her life when she had steeped herself in Marxism, in the Greenwich Village high intellectual life, in a world of Freud and Pavlov and Einstein. She remarked on the tension she had felt between a materialist explanation for our inclinations or actions and another way of understanding them.

"Perhaps you think [I certainly did] that idealism is the *result* of something, the expression of what has happened to a person over time. I think idealism is a result, too, but it's an *inspiration* we receive. I think it's a gift. We have the responsibility of treasuring the gift, though we fail often and take the gift for granted or forget that we have it, that it's been offered to us. You keep talking about secular idealism, but I don't draw that distinction in my mind – between secular idealism and an idealism in the service of God. I don't think God is so jealous about our worship of Him that He will want to separate those who serve His purposes, serve His goodness, because they have read a book, even one written by an atheist, and have been moved, or because they have wanted to be fair all their lives, but have never stepped in a church, from those who have heard God's words in church or read His words in the Bible and have become convinced by them."

A pause, a considerable pause; I was touched, yet again, by her kindness toward others, her refusal to retreat into the ideological confines of a particular world. For some reason, though (my own lack of charity, my cynical nature), I couldn't let the matter drop. I broke the magic, the truth of silence. I was having trouble accepting her broad moral sensibility at face value and appreciating her loving-kindness which extended a wide embrace toward others. I reminded her of what she had already said. "But you didn't always feel as you do now?"

Surprised at my own words, I began to fumble, to qualify. "I mean, it's harder when we're young to be understanding of others – I think for most of us, usually." My eyes were looking at the dark and dusty floor. She kept looking past me at the sky, her mind in a bit of reverie.

"I *was* different then. It's true, we were all caught up in our hopes, our ideals, and we weren't sitting in a room, like you and I are now, wondering about each other's beliefs. Oh, we had those beliefs, and maybe too many of them went unquestioned. I think young people who are going to challenge a powerful nation aren't the ones to keep having doubts about what they believe. Today, as I look back at us, I realize that we were probably narrow at times; we saw what *we* saw and weren't trying to put on the glasses other people were wearing. You're right to remind me of those days — what a tight clan of true believers we were. But they were happy and lively times, often — the excitement, and the energy we found for ourselves. And we paid attention to what was happening. We read the papers carefully, and we were alert — we tried to be alert, we wanted to be alert — to what was happening to people, to poor people, all over the world. It is patting ourselves on the back for me to say so, but I think we really did try to understand how the different economic systems work, and the politics of our nation, and we wanted to see America change, *really* change, and we were going to do something about it."

She stopped abruptly, and I had nothing more to ask or say. She had some tea on a nearby table, which she concluded to be cooled off enough to start sipping. We drifted into an apparently aimless discussion of teas and their variety and of coffee and her lifelong passion for it. That evening I read once more her chapter "A Time of Searching" in *The Long Loneliness*. The description of her life in Chicago during her early twenties held my attention, especially her remarks about "the workers' meetings" which she liked to attend, often held in Lincoln Park on Sundays.

This was not just a social gathering, people of one nationality or background coming together for recreation. They were coming to listen to long and tiresome speeches. They were part of a movement, a slow upheaval. Among them was a stirring and a groping and they were beginning to feel within themselves a power and a possibility. "There can be no revolution without a theory of revolution," Lenin said. They were listening to the theory of revolution. They were pondering their dignity as men, their responsibilities, their hunger for freedom as well as bread.[10]

I wondered whether those men and women were as theoretically disposed as she asserted, even as I wondered whether she herself, at the time, had been so disposed. I listened to some tapes I had with me of young civil rights activists who were struggling to figure out what ought to be done in the South of the early 1960s and what they themselves ought to do with the years immediately ahead of them. Their idealism was strong and connected to a particular historical moment, but they were also eager to develop for themselves a larger sense of what mattered, "an overview," one of them kept saying, his way of referring to "the theory of revolution" Dorothy Day had mentioned.

The next day, now in the morning, with hot coffee, we listened to that particular young, white, Alabama youth talk about his involvement in the civil rights movement and his life as he had experienced it so far and as he hoped to experience it. She was much intrigued. She began to talk, thinking back to her own youthful days, again in Chicago.[11]

"I was very caught up in socialist convictions. I've always believed that people would share with each other, and that for a few to be rich and many to be poor is wrong, dead wrong. Back then I didn't quote from the Bible as much as I do now, but I did read the Bible, even in my most *political* times, when most of my friends were Communists and Socialists. (I think I called them radical friends in the section of *The Long Loneliness* where I discuss my Chicago days.) The Bible isn't meant to keep people apart; it isn't meant to be a badge of honor.

To wear the Bible as a badge of honor is to use it, well, ironically. I feel stronger than that, actually; to clutch at the Bible and dismiss others who don't read it or haven't read it, as 'bad' people or as unworthy, not up to membership in your club, not good enough to be your friends and your allies and comrades – it's sacrilegious to be like that."

She could see by the look on my face that I was puzzled by her use of the word *sacrilegious*. She decided to give me a bit of a lecture.

"The worst sin is pride, and you can have a religious pride that is sinful. I didn't see that for a long time – the way religion can be used to hurt people. I knew history – all the hate in the name of religion: Catholics and Protestants fighting, and Christians and Jews, and Christians and Mohammedans, and Jews and Mohammedans. But in my everyday life, even before I became a Catholic, I had assumed that people who take the time to read the Bible and to pray were going to behave better toward other people, because they would be influenced by all the wonderful poetry in that book. But I was naive, maybe blind. I think the first clue I had about the Bible as a weapon was given me one day in Chicago when I heard a man preaching it, and he seemed without love, completely without love. He was shouting away, cursing away, denouncing all of us 'heathens,' and I felt sorry for him. I listened to him; I kept standing there. I think I wanted to see a smile cross his face. I was hoping he would laugh, maybe. If I had been praying then, as I do now, I would have prayed for him to relax and try to be friendly to people. Maybe I *was* praying for him then, in my own way. Does God have a set way of prayer, a way that He expects each of us to follow? I doubt it. I believe some people – lots of people – pray through the witness of their lives, through the work they do, the friendships they have, the love they offer people and receive from people. Since when are *words* the only acceptable form of prayer?

"I'm not finishing my thought. I was trying to say that a person can be self-righteous about his own righteousness; a person can use the Bible to bring more fear and hate in the world. That's why I think we have to be very careful with the words *secular* and *religious*; you distinguish between them when you ask me your questions, and I know in my mind (I know intellectually) the difference between the two words, what each of them suggests. But, speaking for myself, I'm not so sure that my idealism, back then, was secular; and I'm not so sure that my idealism right now is only a religious kind of interest in helping others who are in a bad jam. The longer I live, the more I see God at work in people who don't have the slightest interest in religion and never read the Bible and wouldn't know what to do if they were persuaded to go inside a church. I always knew how much I admired certain men and women (my 'radical friends') who were giving their lives to help others get a better break; but now I realize how spiritual some of them were, and I'm ashamed of myself for not realizing that long ago, when I was with them, talking and having supper and making our plans, as we did."

She seemed to turn inward, as her eyes stared outward toward the window, which the rain was pelting noisily. I told her that she was probably no less appreciative of her friends back then, in the 1920s, than she would be at the moment we were talking, were they all to appear there before us in that room. She was not comforted by my comment. In fact, she was annoyed. Her eyes left the window, glanced at me for a second or two and then focused on the floor near her feet. Soon she was watching her feet as they stirred just a bit, and I was feeling anxious to break what was clearly a developing silence. She reached for that coffee mug of hers. I noticed that it was empty, which gave me something to say.

"Can I go get you more coffee?"

"No, no thank you."

"I'll be glad to go."

"No, it's all right. I'll wait for soup." Lunch was an hour away. "I was thinking . . ."

But I couldn't remember what I had been thinking. I felt reprimanded by this spell of silence – told that somehow I had missed a point that was made. But I was wrong. She coughed, blew her nose, looked at the coffee mug as if she might be having second thoughts, then abruptly began talking just as I was getting ready to repeat my offer.

"I'm sorry to be so confused on all this. I spent too long being young, and now, even when I'm old, I find myself thinking a lot about young people and what they should do with their lives. My grandchildren have been an influence on me (I keep thinking of them) and we have so many young people come here, and they are all struggling *so hard* to do some good in this world, and it doesn't take much to get into long, long talks with them about . . . well, about *everything*. When I go to bed and lie there, waiting for sleep to take me away, I think of those young people, and something one of them has said to me earlier that day will come back, and I'll wonder whether I said the right thing or whether I should have said something I didn't say. The next morning I'll wake up, and I'll remember a dream I've had – and nothing gets my dreams going like those talks with our young [Catholic Worker] people here. Some of them remind me of my old friends, of me and my doubts and my determination to do *something*. I was restless, *so* restless. But maybe restlessness means somebody is pushing you, reminding you what needs doing.

"I have to keep reminding visitors that many of the young people who come here aren't Catholic, aren't religious at all – they tell you so in no uncertain words. They say they are here to work with us, but we must not (dear God, no!) say they're Catholics or even Christians or practicing Jews or whatever we might think they are. I always tell them the same thing; I say that we are not asking people to fill out membership cards here, and we're not interested in declarations of religious affiliation.

I tell them that we are here to feed the hungry and offer any help we can to anyone who comes to us. One student from an Ivy League college told me that he wondered about the difference between us and the Salvation Army. I felt my face get hot. I knew he had touched on my pride, and I knew I had better watch my every word. He'd been reading *Major Barbara* in a literature course, and he wondered whether . . . Oh, I think he had an idea I might be an elderly Major Barbara, an American general, perhaps, of the Salvation Army, who used a disguise, Catholicism.

"When I felt the blood leaving my cheeks I made them smile, and I told him that we asked no questions here and gave no sermons. I was all set to explain to him what we believed, when I caught myself, just as my mouth was opening up and some sentence was ready to come out. (I'll never know what I would have said to him, because we don't know, a lot of the time, what we're going to say until we say it; we have a general idea only, I think.) My intention was, originally, to tell him about our Catholic Worker philosophy, but I realized in the nick of time that if I did that, gave him a speech, even a short one, he'd have his worst fears confirmed: I would be the Major Barbara he half expected me to be. So I said very little, almost nothing. I told him how we work here, how the cooking and the serving get done, and I said we are grateful for any help we can get, from anyone who comes here and wants to help us. He kept staring at me, right into my eyes, and I tried to look right back and not shift my glance, for fear he would think I wasn't telling him *all*. Then he thanked me, and the next thing I knew, he was trying to cut some celery and potatoes and not doing as good a job, right off, as he may have thought he could do. I think I took some satisfaction in his clumsiness – my pride. I thought to myself, 'They don't teach them how to make soup at Yale or Harvard. Dorothy, your tongue is wicked; mind your manners,' I told myself. I prayed that night at vespers for the young man and for me, I have to admit it; for me because he'd taught me something I knew but needed to keep knowing through being

31

reminded: that there *is* pride in us, even when we're fighting it, and that there is a Major Barbara side to a lot of us – I should say, to me.

"That night I had one of those dreams I was telling you about, and that young man was in it. He was in a pulpit, in an Episcopal church, not a Catholic one. I know, because I was sitting in the pew, and I saw the Book of Common Prayer, and I picked it up and started flipping through the pages, and I came upon a page that had a section from John, the fourth chapter, one I have always loved, and I remember my mother loving it: 'Let us love one another, for love is of God; and everyone that loveth is born of God, and knoweth God. He that loveth not knoweth not God; for God is love.' I'm sure those words *are* in the Book of Common Prayer, though I don't have a copy now.

"I just sat in the pew with those words going through me, and then the minister came, and he walked up the stairs and stood in the pulpit, and opened the Bible there and started reading from it, and what a strange coincidence: he read the same words, the same ones, from John; and then I saw *him*; I mean I noticed who he was, and he was that student, that young man. I think I flushed in my dream. It was then that I woke up."

She was a *little* red in the cheeks, I thought – or maybe I was imagining so, to suit some psychological cleverness, if not wicked-ness, in me. She smiled and reached over with her right hand for her Bible; she put it on her lap and tapped it a few times. I thought she was going to pick it up, open it, find that passage in John, read it to herself, or read it aloud to both of us. But she didn't open the book. "All my life," she said, "I've wondered how God can keep track of everything that happens here, because so much is going on, in everyone's life, and there are hundreds of millions, billions of people, and they keep being born, and they die, and new people are born." She stopped, and I hadn't the slightest notion of what direction her inquiry would next take. A facetious side of me had an "association," as my kind calls it: a heavenly computer of gigantic proportions in constant employ by Him. Enough of a smirk crossed my face for her to take notice, and I said, "It's an enormous amount of information for anyone to digest – all that we human beings do on this planet." Now she smiled, unaware of my amusement, or maybe thoroughly aware.

"It's mind boggling, I know. When my grandchildren were younger they would ask me about that, how the good Lord *ever* manages to keep track of so many of us, and I would tell them I didn't know, and none of us will ever know, and that's what God is, a mystery to us in so many ways. I could see that I wasn't satisfying them with my answer, so I'd tell them that, frankly I wasn't satisfied with what I'd told them, but that there wasn't anything else I knew to say, other than to suggest that we have faith in Him, in God, and hope that He'll help us to answer the questions we want to put to Him. And you know what, it was then, at moments like that, I'd pick up the Bible and read to them from John, the fourth chapter: 'God is love.' They knew what to make of that. They knew how to understand that."

We sat there in quiet agreement, though I can still recall thinking to myself that the assertion "God is love" can all too easily get turned into a secular banality. Dorothy Day had apparently been worrying along similar lines, because she reminded me of this. "I'm afraid some of my agnostic and atheist friends like that chapter from John for the wrong reasons. It's the kind of sentence I have seen on those Unitarian billboards outside a church. God bless the Unitarians – I don't mean to be critical of them, though it's not a religion I was ever going to explore."

She stopped again, seeming to be caught by a memory that wouldn't let go of her. After about five seconds she raised her head toward the ceiling and smiled. "I was remembering my visits to Catholic churches during my young, radical days." In *The Long Loneliness* she makes reference to those visits. In Chicago, and especially in New Orleans, she would stop at a church, sit there, not necessarily say or think or do anything, simply *be*. "I was always dropping into the Cathedral," she tells us in the concluding section of the chapter "A Time of Searching."[12] She was referring to the Catholic church that dominates Jackson Square in New Orleans. Even though a visit to the church calmed her and made her pensive, she balked as well. "I became acquainted with Catholic terminology, which at times seemed strange and even illiterate: 'To make a mission, to pray for someone's intention' – what kind of jargon was this?"[13]

She was "searching," as she put it, but she was also quite sure of her social and political convictions, and in certain important respects they remained constant over the years. Her Chicago imprisonment caused her to feel "shame and regret and self-contempt" – to be kept for days in jail and to be branded publicly as a whore because she had been arrested in a house where IWW people were staying: the presence there of her and her friends meant only one thing to the men who made the arrest, hence their arraignment in a "morals court." In her autobiography she is impatient with herself, and wonders whether she and her women friends hadn't played into the hands of a red-baiting federal authority. (The notorious Palmer raids of the Harding administration were in progress, and, in fact, she had become one victim of that era's seriously flawed justice.) Yet her writing expresses another kind of anguish – her embarrassment as she looked back (in the early 1950s) at her "carelessness of convention," at what she calls "the loose moral standards of the radicals," in whose company, of course, she counted herself.

I had not intended to discuss that aspect of her youth, but she brought up the subject on her own, with less reluctance or embarrassment than I had imagined would be the case were someone to prompt her. We had been talking about the demands a radical life can place on a person, even as a religious life can pose difficult constraints and obligations. Suddenly she made this comment:

"I don't think the moral life of a social activist is a separate
matter; I think we are responsible for how we behave with each

other – [when] making a protest, taking a political stand; and if we exploit each other personally and keep holding our placards and proclaiming our ideals to the world, then we've become hypocrites, and if we don't see what has happened to us, we are *blind* hypocrites. I'm afraid I was in that kind of trouble when I was young."

She pursued that line of reflection.[14]

"I have tried to forget those days, but I never will. When I finished writing about them in *The Long Loneliness*, I thought I was through with them, but we're never through with our lives, I've begun to realize – any part of them. For many young radicals their political protests become so entwined with their personal lives, it's hard to figure which side of them is running the show. I was foolish then; I was caught in stormy love affairs or infatuations; there is no other way to put it. I had no moral bearings – not enough of them, anyway. I remember one woman telling me, in Chicago, that I'd grow up one day, and then I'd settle down and stop being so selfish. I couldn't understand, at the time, what she was talking about. I told her so. 'You will,' she kept saying, and I got angrier and angrier as I listened to her. But she had taken a good hard look, and she knew what she saw – some of us drifting and preventing ourselves from looking at ourselves squarely in the mirror by claiming that the world is a terrible place, and we were going to change it, if only we had the time and some luck working for us.

"The world *was* in terrible shape, and I'm glad we stood up and said what we believed; but a lot of the time we'd say these beautiful things about justice and fairness and equality, but we weren't so nice to each other. We'd be jealous and we'd gossip, and we'd be moody and difficult and rude and inconsiderate. Why do I say 'we'? I mean *I* would be all that – and if at the time I ever came near to knowing what I'd become, I'd dodge, I'd duck, I'd go on the offensive: the terrible Wall Street bankers. Lots of them were terrible – and so were lots of us."

She allowed herself no smile, however slight, to soften the judgment. Later that evening I would read these words in *The Long Loneliness*: "I have long since come to believe that people never mean half of what they say, and that it is best to disregard their talk and judge only their actions." I fear she had in mind some "actions" for which she was not prepared to offer herself forgiveness. She gives hints in her autobiographical writing.

> A man with whom I had been deeply in love for several years was a lover of Pascal, so I became acquainted with his *Pensées*, which I did not understand but which stirred me. This same friend was a reader of Dostoievski, and, whereas I had read him as a matter of routine, because I loved the Russians, now I read him with an understanding of men and suffering. This same man hated James Joyce, the flavor of whose books fascinated me; once when we were riding on a North Avenue elevated, and I was speaking of Joyce to him, he wrestled the book which happened to be *Portrait of the Artist as a Young Man* from my hands and threw it out the window of the train.
>
> And always there was the New Testament. I could not hear of Sonia's reading the gospel to Raskolnikov in *Crime and Punishment* without turning to it myself with love. I could not read Ippolyte's rejection of his ebbing life and defiance of God in *The Idiot* without being filled with an immense gratitude to God for life and a desire to make some return.
>
> The first rosary I ever had was given to me by a friend of my disorderly life . . .[15]

Decades after she wrote these words she was still making recriminations about this "disorderly" life. I decided one morning, as she was being quite candid, to say as much as I found myself able to say on the matter. I began with this comment:[16] "I think I've got a fairly accurate idea of what you regard as your disorderly life from the reading I have done – from reading *The Eleventh Virgin*." I stopped there and saw that she had already absorbed what I intended: my awareness of the autobiographical nature of the novel. She was stern as she looked at me. I was preparing to apologize when a broad smile broke over her face, and she began telling me about one of her old obsessions:

"There was a time that I thought I had a lifetime job cut out for me – to track down every copy of that novel and destroy them all, one by one. I'm as ashamed of *that* as anything: the sin of pride, if there ever was an example of it. I used to lie in bed thinking about the book in all the libraries, and once I even tried to find out how many libraries there are in the country. I knew, of course, that most of them had better things to do with their funds than buy a novel from an unknown writer, but the book was in a few libraries, and my hope was to get rid of it as completely as I could.

"Once I told a priest in confession what I was trying to do. He laughed. He said, 'My, my.' I thought he was going to tell me to stop being so silly and mixed up in my priorities. Two of my best friends had told me they thought I needed a psychiatrist. But I will remember to my last day here on God's earth what that priest said: 'You can't have much faith in God if you're taking the life He has given you and using it that way.' I didn't say a word in reply. He added, 'God is the one who forgives us, if we ask Him; and it sounds like you don't even want forgiveness – just to get rid of the books.' Then he went on to quote to me from that haunting second letter Paul wrote to the people of Corinth: 'Ye are our epistle written in our hearts, known and read by all men: forasmuch as ye are [manifestly] declared to be the epistle of Christ ministered by us, written not with ink, but with the Spirit of the living God; not in tables of stone, but in fleshy tables of the heart.'

"I left that confessional booth feeling stupid. I began to realize how wrapped up I had become in myself, in my words, in my reputation that I had been worrying and worrying about: what people would think of me, *if* . . . *if* they got their hands on that book. I took one of the longest walks of my life; I kept hearing that priest's words. Usually I never have wondered what the priest *looks* like, who has heard my confession, but that time I did. It was as if he had come to know me better than I ever dreamed I'd know myself, and I wanted to make him as real as possible in my mind – connect his voice to a picture of him, so there would be less chance that I'd forget what he said to me.

"Since then I still think of that book of mine. I still hope that no one who hasn't read it ever will. But I'm not as worried as I used to be, and with each year I forget more and more. But you can't forget your life, and even if God has forgiven you (and no one can dare *assume* He has) what was wrong was wrong, and we have our memories for a reason – to learn from our mistakes and not keep repeating them. I hope I've learned, and I hope I won't forget what my mistakes ended up teaching me – what the priest pointed out: the vanity or pride at work in my heart."

I tried to mobilize one of those "contexts" psychiatrists are so fond of supplying. I described the emotional and sexual trials and turmoils I had noticed among young civil rights workers – not a function of their wickedness or their peculiar psychiatric difficulties, I carefully explained, but a consequence of their age, their struggles as young men and women to figure out this life, to find a particular place for themselves in the world with a particular person.[17] Dorothy Day nodded politely, but I could tell that she wasn't impressed by the "developmental" rationale I was peddling.

It was at moments like this that I felt most estranged from her, thinking of my own life as well as that of my children and my students. She may have had reason to berate herself for her earlier life, the petty jealousies and the self-centeredness which a series of affairs no doubt prompted. Yet she hadn't been just "floundering," as she put it, nor "sinning," either. Like so many young activists she was trying to be true to herself and to her ideals and to learn more about what the word *love* means. I never dared ask her directly what I wanted to put to her – whether she really wanted to see our young people leap from high school into marriage, or for that matter – and just as important – into a monastery. I alluded to this matter once or twice, pointed out that the so-called sexual revolution wasn't all that bad — that it had its positive side and spared us, maybe, some marriages that were never meant to be and prepared the way for other strong, enduring marriages. However, she would have none of my modernist apologias. "I think the church is wise to insist upon restraint," she told me one time, and her face indicated quickly that there would be a (painful) silence: next subject, please.

On another occasion she went so far as to acknowledge that at Catholic Worker meetings, in Catholic Worker settings of various kinds, she had seen "the unholy alliance," she called it, of a decent commitment to eminently worthwhile objectives living side by side with what she had to call sinfulness. Such sinfulness, she hastened to add, is not confined to any kind of person — young or old, idealistic or utterly materialistic. But she was not willing to justify it, as I was, through the great contemporary pardon psychiatry offers.

"I still think that we have to hold up certain standards for ourselves and not put them aside, because God is the one whose judgment really counts. He is judging over the longest haul, but He depends on you and me to take a hard look at ourselves, and so I shouldn't forget His forgiveness as a *hope*, but I shouldn't treat His forgiveness as if it was part of a bank account I have, and I can just keep drawing on it, whenever I feel I want to do so. When I see a person being idealistic one minute and tripping someone walking down the aisle the next, I feel my temper rising. I try to ask for God's help, but it doesn't always come — maybe because He wants me to go right ahead and say what's on my mind. (Who can ever know what is on *His* mind?) Anyway, I have had some harsh looks to give people, and muttered some cold, cold words to people, and I've been wrong many times, but not always, I would guess."

She wasn't slyly boasting; she was struggling, still, with her own past life. She was even, on yet another occasion, willing to be a little "psychological"[18] herself, as she thought about her social and political struggles when she was a young woman and her not very happy love affairs.

> "We got so worked up, fighting causes that weren't easy to fight, unpopular causes, with the whole weight of the society against us. We weren't martyrs, I don't mean that – but we were taking chances, and we ended up in jail a few times. No wonder we reached out for affection and solace. I don't think we need Freud to explain what happens to people when they're under great pressure and they only have each other's company."

Here she seemed to be reminding herself that young human relatedness, including its sexual aspect, and idealism need not be exempt from charity. As she thought of those moments of political and moral affirmation, she remembered their personal cost: the tears and the pain, the confinement, the jeopardy – and with all that, the closeness, the camaraderie, and more. Mistakes there were, there are, there will be. But, she added, "The biggest mistake, sometimes, is to play things very safe in this life and end up being moral failures." We didn't have time to continue. She wanted to help with the soup line that had formed early, for it was an unusually cold morning. As we set a time to meet again, her last words set me thinking about her conversion, about a wager (in the Pascalian sense) between "playing things safe" or taking a very big chance indeed.

Conversion

Dramatic moments of religious conversion have always commanded attention from a public eager for the unusual, the surprising. I remember a lecture by Paul Tillich[1] on religious biography, which he began by mocking himself: "There are those who wonder whether I'll ever experience a conversion." Then, this celebrated Christian theologian – who recognized that for many his ideas had the distinct ring of culturally sanctioned agnosticism – continued with an examination of various "conversions," which he concluded by saying, "I think most conversions are gradual – the culmination of years of faith, which a person has finally given the credibility of an acceptance in public of religious membership."

At the time, I chafed at his use of the word *credibility*, as if all one's private moments of worship or reflection needed credibility or a gesture. But he was simply pointing out that most of us don't suddenly feel impelled to change.

Dorothy Day has given us abundant evidence in her autobiography and letters and columns that she was for many years drawn to church visits and church services. These spiritual interests also emerge in her great affection for the Russian novelists Tolstoy and Dostoievski, her interest in the Hebrew prophets, and her friendships with Jewish writers such as Mike Gold, who may have renounced Judaism as a religion, but whose secular righteousness had important Jewish sources of inspiration. Extensive passages of *The Long Loneliness* tell of her religious yearnings, even while she was in her politically radical and ostensibly agnostic or atheist period.

Her formal religious life began in the middle 1920s, when she was about twenty-seven or twenty-eight and involved in a fulfilling involvement with Forster Batterham. "The man I loved, with whom I entered into a common-law marriage, was an anarchist, an Englishman by descent, and a biologist." This was her way of starting a chapter in the autobiography titled "Man Is Meant for Happiness."[2] She makes it quite clear that the two of them were enormously happy with one another and that for a long time there seemed no likelihood that they would ever leave one another. And yet how "happy" were they? Were there tensions before the baby Tamar was conceived? (Forster had no wish to have children, but when the time came, he did not shirk from a father's responsibilities.) Why did a woman like Dorothy Day take up with a man who made clear his atheism, a man for whom science meant so much, and religion so little? Out of love, of course, one answers, as she answered in her chapter. She describes that love, their long walks, and all that he taught her about the natural world. She had, at last, found "peace." But, she writes, "It was a peace, curiously enough, divided against itself. I was happy but my very happiness made me know there was a greater happiness to be obtained from life than any I had ever known. I began to think, to weigh things, and it was at this time that I began consciously to pray more."[3]

Why should happiness, at last achieved, prompt such an inquiry, such weighing and praying? Why should natural happiness, as she calls it in her book, lead to an intensified effort to come into contact with the greater happiness of the supernatural? Such questions, these days, might lead to psychological explanations. In Pascal's day, or Saint Augustine's (not to mention that of Saint Teresa of Avila) they might have seemed as natural as the happiness Dorothy Day described.[4] On a snowy February day in 1973, I decided to risk putting them to her, perhaps because I sensed that they need not be considered irreverent or insulting, but rather natural.[5]

"I was reading your chapter on the happiness you felt when you met Forster, and I noted that you began consciously to pray more at that time, and I wondered why."

She looked right at me and didn't hesitate long before she replied,

"I don't think prayer for me has only been connected with sadness and misery. I have prayed when I have felt low and tired and worried. But when I have felt joy and fulfillment in this world I have always wanted to say thank you. I just can't believe there isn't someone to thank. I remember when I was a child, and I'd wish something would happen, and it did, I would try to find a minute to whisper thank you. I wasn't thanking my mother and my father – I was thanking the God of fate and chance, I suppose, the way children do: Lady Luck, or my good-luck charm, or the little piece of rabbit fur my younger brother carried on his keychain. Now I hope you don't jump on me and tell me I was being superstitious then, and I'm being superstitious now. I was being *thankful*. I felt thankful when I met Forster and fell in love with him, and he fell in love with me. I wanted to express my thanks. I told him that – how grateful I felt to be with him. He was glad to hear of my affection and gratitude, but he had no sense of there being anyone to thank. That was the point of our eventual disagreement, our separation. It wasn't something we could really argue over, though we did. If a person wants to pour out her gratitude to the universe, and someone else has no desire to do that and finds such a desire foolish or absurd, then there is going to be a reckoning, or maybe they'll just agree to disagree. We *did*, as a matter of fact. That's how we lived together without much trouble at all – until our daughter was born."

She did not say anything more. She kept looking directly at me, though. By then I had realized, after months of conversations, that when she really wanted to stop a line of conversation or inquiry she looked noticeably, pointedly away – over my shoulder, into the distance; or she stared at the floor and moved invisible objects to and fro with her feet; or else she simply changed the subject drastically by asking a question or making a statement that had us on quite a different tack, as in, "I've been thinking that we haven't discussed . . ." Now she seemed to be awaiting any further comments I might have to make or questions to ask. But I was mute. Finally, before serving lunch to the line of waiting people, she asked me if I had anything more to ask. I told her no, not right then, but I did remember one passage in *The Long Loneliness* about which I wanted to ask her at some point, and would she mind if I read it to her? No, of course not. I then read these lines:

Forster, the inarticulate, became garrulous only in wrath. And his wrath, he said, was caused by my absorption in the supernatural rather than the natural, the unseen rather than the seen.

He had always rebelled against the institution of the family and the tyranny of love. It was hard for me to see at such times why we were together, since he lived with me as though he were living alone and he never allowed me to forget that this was a comradeship rather than a marriage.

She shifted her position in the chair and cleared her throat. I felt embarrassed, even rude. In an effort to change the subject, I asked if we might change an appointment we had made and explained why. She was cordial and obliging, but then she quickly returned to the subject of Forster.

"I was happy, but there were moments when I was unhappy as well. We were two stubborn individuals, I guess. Forster had no interest in religion; it was nonsense or worse, so far as he was concerned. I had a strong interest in religion. I knew of his views; he knew of mine. I don't know what would have happened to either of us if the other had given in on the subject of God. I am not sure Forster would have respected me, had I yielded to his viewpoint. He placed *such* store in a person's obligation to live up to his beliefs. If he had come over to my

way of seeing the world, with God as its guiding spirit, I might
have lived a completely different life than the one I did.
I guess you'd not be sitting here now; I guess there would be
no 'here', now, if you know what I mean."

I did, and for the first time I began to understand another sentence
of *The Long Loneliness* that I had often questioned: "I had known
Forster a long time before we contracted our common-law relationship, and I have always felt that it was life with him that brought
me natural happiness, that brought me to God." She seems to mean
a gradual ascent: first the shared love and commitment with another
person which lifted her out of a period of aimlessness and drifting;
then the spiritual knowledge and passion which gradually became
stronger, until she had two anchors, the common-law marriage and
the active, intense religious life she pursued and then found; and
then the shift to making religion the central concern of her life. Yet
her own account, in the chapter "Having a Baby" of *The Long
Loneliness*, makes quite clear that this ascent was not smooth. She
went through an exceedingly difficult time with Forster and with
herself as she shifted from the secular to the religious life. After
telling her readers how much happiness she had come to know as a
result of her love for Forster and his for her, she opens the chapter
on a curiously melancholy note: "I was surprised that I found myself
beginning to pray daily. I could not get down on my knees, but I
could pray while I was walking. If I got down on my knees, I thought,
Do I really believe? Whom am I praying to? A terrible doubt came
over me, and a sense of shame, and I wondered if I was praying
because I was lonely, because I was unhappy."

Those are not the usual words of a newlywed settling into natural
happiness. She mentions, in the next paragraph, that she prayed
as she went to the village for her mail, that she held in her pocket
the rosary given her in New Orleans, that she even tried reciting
the rosary. She also tells us that she sometimes turned on herself,
mocked her religious interests and beliefs, and recited the scornful
slogans her atheist and radical friends were wont to hurl at others,
particularly "Religion is the opiate of the people."

In this period, she wrote, she was "in a stupor of content," and her prayers were meant to keep her there, or, indeed, had got her there in the first place. However, as one moves through this stirring, unsettling chapter, it becomes clear that she was not really in a stupor, benign or otherwise. She was lonely, a bit unnerved, self-deprecating, and prone to moodiness. "Forster was in the city all week, coming out weekends. I finished the writing I was doing and felt at loose ends, thinking enviously of my friends going gaily about the city, about their work, with plenty of companionship." She calls herself, a bit further on, a sybaritic anchorite, yet makes clear that she had plenty to do and friends whom she valued right there on Staten Island. Nor is she fooled by the prospect of a return to the Manhattan life she knew so well.

> In spite of my desire for a sociable week in town, in spite of a de-sire to pick up and flee from my solitude, I took joy in thinking of the idiocy of the pleasures I would indulge in if I were there. Cocktail parties, with prohibition drinks, dinners, the conversa-tion or lack of it, dancing in a smoky crowded room when one might be walking on the beach, the dull, restless cogitations which come after dissipating one's energies – things which struck me with renewed force every time I spent days in the city.

The tugging between her past life and her ongoing life filled her with mixed feelings: the city or the country; a cosmopolitan culture or a relatively simple small-town one; to be alone or in the company of others; to be politically engaged or preoccupied with a more private life. But such clearcut polarities are perhaps less important than an underlying anguish that can be felt in her prose, written long after the time of life being recalled. Despite the happiness she keeps mentioning, she doesn't look back at those days with nostal-gia. She was candid about the trouble brought into her relationship with Forster by her growing religious sensibility. "But it was impos-sible to talk about religion or faith to him. A wall immediately separated us. The very love of nature, and the study of her secrets which was bringing me to faith, cut Forster off from religion."

In time, clearly, the two of them had to come to terms with conflict in their shared life, and we all know the outcome. Though life with Forster brought Dorothy Day to God and enabled her to enter the Catholic church, it was this very faith that ended their relationship.

But first their child, Tamar Teresa, was born. The prospect of having a child brought great joy to Day; she had believed herself to be unfruitful, barren. But the response of the future child's father was different. "There were conflicts because Forster did not believe in bringing children into such a world as we lived in." She goes further, at another point: "His fear of responsibility, his dislike of having the control of others, his extreme individualism made him feel that he of all men should not be a father."

This difference of opinion was only the beginning of a struggle. During her pregnancy Dorothy Day prayed constantly. She also read the *Imitation of Christ*.[6] Moreover, she kept merging in her mind the arrival of her child, its baptism, and her own eventual entrance into the Catholic church. "I knew that I was going to have my child baptized, cost what it may," she observes in the "Having a Baby" chapter of *The Long Loneliness*. She continues, "I knew that I was not going to have her floundering through many years as I had done, doubting and hesitating, undisciplined and amoral." A page or two on she makes clear in two sentences how the fate of her common-law marriage and of her daughter's future religious life and her own, too, all hung in the balance at that time. "There had been the physical struggle, the mortal combat, almost, of giving birth to a child, and now there was coming the struggle for my own soul. Tamar would be baptized, and I knew the rending it would cause in human relations around me."

Matters did, indeed, deteriorate, as she makes clear in a chapter ironically titled "Love Overflows." Tamar was baptized in July of 1927, and her mother narrates the consequences in a description of what was supposed to be a celebration afterward.

We came back to the beach house to a delightful lunch of boiled lobsters and salad. Forster had caught the lobsters in his traps for the feast and then did not remain to partake of it. He left, not returning for several days. It was his protest against my yearnings toward the life of the spirit, which he considered a morbid escapism. He exulted in his materialism . . . Forster saw man in the light of reason and not in the light of faith. He had thought of the baptism only as a mumbo jumbo, the fuss and flurry peculiar to women. At first he had been indulgent and had brought in the lobsters for the feast. And then he had become angry with some sense of the end to which all this portended. Jealousy set in and he left me.

As a matter of fact, he left me quite a number of times that coming winter and following summer, as he felt my increasing absorption in religion. The tension between us was terrible.

She would eventually become ill, and soon enough the end of their "marriage" would take place:

I became so oppressed I could not breathe and I awoke in the night choking. I was weak and listless and one doctor told me my trouble was probably thyroid. I went to the Cornell clinic for a metabolism test and they said my condition was a nervous one. By winter the tension had become so great that an explosion occurred and we separated again. When he returned, as he always had, I would not let him in the house; my heart was breaking with my own determination to make an end, once and for all, to the torture we were undergoing.

The next day, she adds immediately, she was "baptized conditionally" (she had been baptized in the Episcopal church many years earlier), and she also made "first confession right afterward," and would, the following morning, receive Communion.

Before this crisis between them Dorothy Day acknowledges that Forster – no matter his abstract objection about bringing children into the world – had become a loving, caring father. She was also well aware of what effect her conversion would have on their personal life. "Only the baby interested him. She was his delight. Which made it, of course, the harder to contemplate the cruel blow I was going to strike him when I became a Catholic." Forster had been severely depressed then – "stricken over the tragedy" of the execution of Sacco and Vanzetti. She tells us that he "did not eat for days," and that he "sat around the house in a stupor of misery." Once (she mentions this several times) he had managed to "take refuge in nature as being more kindly, more beautiful and peaceful than the world of men." But not at this point in this life. "Now he could not even escape through nature as he tried to escape so many problems in life."

The major problem he could not escape, surely, was the breakup of the love affair – and the friendship – which mattered so much to him. Moreover, his love for his daughter was growing constantly. Even Dorothy Day's close Catholic friends and spiritual confidantes were loath to encourage her to convert right after Tamar was born. They were aware of the meaning a father has to a child and that since Forster was to become a father, he would be a far better one if he spent time getting to know his young child. He was, in his own way, grieving not only the death of Sacco and Vanzetti, but his own impending demise as a husband and father.

Dorothy Day claims in "Love Overflows" that she did everything possible to avert such an outcome.

> We both suffered in body as well as in soul and mind. He would not talk about the faith and relapsed into complete silence if I tried to bring up the subject. The point of my bringng it up was that I could not become a Catholic and continue living with him, because he was averse to any ceremony before officials of either church or state. He was an anarchist and an atheist, and he did not intend to be a liar or a hypocrite. He was a creature of utter sincerity, and however illogical and bad-tempered about it all, I loved him. It was killing me to think of leaving him.

In a moving passage she spells out her love in its daily reality:

Fall nights we read a great deal. Sometimes he went out to dig
bait if there was a low tide and the moon was up. He stayed
out late on the pier fishing, and came in smelling of seaweed
and salt air; getting into bed, cold with the chill November air,
he held me close to him in silence. I loved him in every way, as
a wife, as a mother even. I loved him for all he knew and pitied
him for all he didn't know. I loved him for the odds and ends I
had to fish out of his sweater pockets and for the sand and
shells he brought in with his fishing. I loved his lean cold body
as he got into bed smelling of the sea, and I loved his integrity
and stubborn pride.

In the end, though, she loved the Catholic church more. After
she had been formally baptized, she describes her participation in
the rituals of prayer. At first they took place "grimly, coldly." She
wondered what she was doing, whether she had become duped by
"an opiate, the opiate of the people." She felt "like a hypocrite"
when she was on her knees in prayer, and she "shuddered at the
thought of anyone" catching sight of her. On the other hand, she
wanted desperately to be the most devout and prayerful and faithful
Catholic possible. "I wanted to be poor, chaste, and obedient. I
wanted to die in order to live, to put off the old man and put on
Christ. I loved, in other words, and like all women in love, I wanted
to be united to my love." She was able to see what this passion
had done to her earlier life, now ending. "Why should not Forster
be jealous? Any man who did not participate in this love would,
of course, realize my infidelity, my adultery. In the eyes of God,
any turning toward creatures to the exclusion of Him is adultery,
and so it is termed over and over again in Scripture."

She had married into the church, then, by her own description;
not as a nun does, for she was hardly eligible for that vocation,
but as her own kind of lay convert, and she was ready to give
herself, voluntarily, body and mind and soul to an institution, no
matter the doubts weighing on her. There are, in *The Long Loneliness*, some of the triumphal sounds one encounters in the literature

of conversion – as in, say, Thomas Merton's *The Seven Storey Mountain*. In all these stories, a troubled and hurt person who has tried many ways of living, who has gone from secular faith to secular faith (whether it is Marx, Freud, consumerism, or debauchery) ends up in the arms of the church and suddenly cannot understand how others, outside, can possibly still be standing where they are, can still fail to see the Light of the World. But in *The Long Loneliness* the religious sentimentality is more than matched, on important occasions, by a self-scrutinizing skepticism that allowed her to talk about the sinful aspect of her self-absorption. She was able to make devastating observations, at the very time of her conversion, about the very church she chose to embrace in a full, passionate marriage. "I loved the Church for Christ made visible," she observes immediately after she describes her personal vow to be "poor, chaste, and obedient" as a Catholic. She then adds this stinging remark on almost two thousand years of Church history: "Not for itself [did she love it], because it was so often a scandal to me. Romano Guardini said the Church is the Cross on which Christ was crucified; one could not separate Christ from His cross, and one must live in a state of permanent dissatisfaction with the Church."[7]

There were, as is so often the case, people who were ready to use her conversion for their own purposes, supposedly Christian in nature. "Not long [after I had converted], a priest wanted me to write a story of my conversion, telling how the social teaching of the church had led me to embrace Catholicism. But I knew nothing of the social teaching of the church at that time. I had never heard of the encyclicals." Her conversion was not political, she kept saying as we talked. She could understand, though, how today people might think in those terms, given her own life before the conversion and the life of the church in the last few decades, as it has taken on various social and economic problems. At the same time she did not want to get, as she once put it, "too psychological" about the conversion, despite her own suggestive comments about its connection to her daughter's birth and her common-law husband's view of the world.

When I inquired, during our conversations, what she felt were her "rock-bottom reasons" for entering the church at that time, she replied,

"I don't know exactly how to answer you. I sometimes forget that I was once not Catholic. The church has meant so much to me for so long, I can't conceive of life without it – and yet, for about three decades, that's how I lived. When I converted, some of my friends thought I had *stopped* living. Oh, they thought I had lost my mind. They thought I had been drugged by someone, they didn't know who. And they couldn't accuse Forster, so they were looking all over for someone to call the devil. Once – I'll never forget the moment, while we sat and ate supper – Forster talked a little about religion, by asking me a question. He wanted to know, well, these were his words: 'Who is it, pushing you to the Catholics?' I was surprised; I was so taken aback I didn't know what to answer. I sat there, and now *I* was silent. He stared at me, and I could see that my silence made him extremely suspicious. He knew there was no other man; but then, I realized that there *was* another man, because God had become man and visited us and called each of us to Him, and so I said that to him; I said, 'It is Jesus. I guess it is Jesus Christ who is the one who is pushing me to the Catholics, because their church is His Church; He chose it.'

"He turned white as I never had seen him, and I expected him to get up and walk out and not be back here for a while. When he got angry, that's what he did – turn white and silent, and then he would just disappear. He would sometimes sleep on the beach and live on the beach; he would become even more a part of the natural world than he usually was. But this time he didn't move. He sat there and glared at me. I asked him whether we could talk some more about religion, now that he had asked me that question, and I thanked him for asking me. He didn't say a word, and he didn't nod or shake his head, and he would do one or the other sometimes when he felt moody and unwilling – I guess you would say unable – to talk. He just looked at me, and I got nervous. I thought he was in trouble and might 'take a fit'; that was an expression I would hear my mother use when I was a girl. She would say, "Be careful, or so-and-so will take a fit.'

"At last Forster stopped staring at me; he looked down at his hands, and he then clasped them together, the way a child does, sometimes, in school, when he's trying to show the teacher he's a good boy: he clasps his hands together and puts them on the desk and sits there and waits for instructions on what to do next. For seconds and seconds he sat like that, and I started getting nervous again. I think I could feel the angry energy in him. Then he lifted his hands up – keeping them clasped – and pounded them down hard on the table, and the dishes rattled, and I wondered what he would do next. I had an awful thought cross my mind: that he would get up now and lose control and start hitting me with his clasped hands. But, of course, he didn't. I was mortified, later, as I thought about the time – that such a thought should cross my mind. I felt that I had been unfair to him in my mind. But he *had* been upset, and after he pounded the table, he got up and he told me that he thought I was either under some spell, or something bad was happening to me, to my mind. I tried to get him to talk more, to talk about *that*, what he had just said, but he wouldn't; he couldn't. He unclasped his hands and he just walked once around the table, and the next thing I knew, he was gone."

She stopped there and seemed not to want to continue. Why didn't I speak up and say what not only the psychiatrist in me wondered, but what I believe many of us, deeply respectful of her, nevertheless have wondered: Was there something in Forster, aside from his lack of interest in religion, even enmity toward it, which she found herself wanting to flee? As a friend of mine has put it, "A man who goes out, in his misery, to live on the beach must have had as much of God in him as any of the people Dorothy Day would later care for so patiently." In *The Long Loneliness* she herself acknowledged this. "That conflict was in me. A woman does not feel whole without a man. . . . It was years before I awakened without that longing for a face pressed against my breast, an arm about my shoulder. . . ." Why, then, did she determine upon celibacy as a necessary aspect of her conversion, her new Catholic life, and soon enough, her new Catholic activist life? Such questions raced across my mind, but her expression made me swallow them whole.

She had a hot cup of tea near her and had been waiting for it to cool enough to be drinkable. She tested it, prematurely, I felt, in order to have something to do. It was still hot; I could tell by her hasty retreat. But then she immediately picked it up and took a rather full swig, and with evident pain to her tongue, her throat, and her esophagus, swallowed it in one fast gulp. I sat still and said nothing. I noticed that her hands were clasped and that mine were not because I had been aware of an urge to clasp my hands and had resisted it.

Suddenly she started talking again.

"I don't know what happened to me then. I didn't know how to answer Forster's questions or the questions all my New York City friends – my radical friends, all of whom I loved so much – were asking when the subject of me and my religious interests came up. I think a lot of people wanted me to go see a doctor. One person kept telling me I should find the best alienist in Manhattan. That was an old term for psychiatrist. I told him that I hoped God would forgive him for thinking religion was something crazy, and he got very angry with me. He told me I was in a lot of trouble, and it was the worst kind: because I didn't know it, how much trouble I really had gotten myself in. I laughed and told him he had quite a nice way of thinking going for himself: heads he wins, and tails I lose, because no matter what I would say, he would be telling me that I wasn't aware of what was really going on inside me. He did laugh, then, but some of my other friends weren't going to laugh, even if I tried to make light of what we were talking about: me and my churchgoing. I told one friend that he never minded when I went to lots of parties and drank too much, so why not be glad that I would only take a small sip of wine, if I became a Catholic, at Communion. I didn't like such talk, to be honest, but I thought it was the best way to stop some of those very tough conversations with people who were now looking at me as if I was in lots of trouble."

Another pause.

"I wasn't interested in analyzing myself the way my friends were. After Forster left, that day, I kept thinking to myself that it was hopeless: I believed in Jesus Christ — that He is *real*, that He is the son of God, that He came here, that He entered history, and that He is still here, with us, all the time, through His Church, through the sacraments of the church. But Forster and others believed that something bad had happened to me or that I had fallen by the wayside, probably because my psychological problems were extremely serious. I *did* ask myself if I thought something was wrong with me, but I wasn't convinced. I felt that I was being *saved* from wrong, not that something *was* wrong."

In her autobiography she acknowledges moments of self-doubt, even *after* her conversion.

I had no particular joy in partaking of these three sacraments, Baptism, Penance and Holy Eucharist. I proceeded about my own active participation in them . . . making acts of faith, and certainly with no consolation whatever. One part of my mind stood at one side and kept saying, "What are you doing? Are you sure of yourself? What kind of affectation is this? What act is this you are going through? Are you trying to induce emotion, induce faith, partake of an opiate, the opiate of the people?" I felt like a hypocrite if I got down on my knees, and shuddered at the thought of anyone seeing me.

She is more critical of herself than she may have realized when she wrote these words and noticed this in our conversations two decades later. She brought up repeatedly the comments others have made about *The Long Loneliness.*

"I have received letters over the years about that book, and most of them have been friendly and complimentary, but not all. The critical letters still tell me the same thing – that I have bought into hogwash, as one colorful-talking man from Oklahoma told me. (I think he was from Oklahoma City.) He wanted me to buy into a Protestant sect. He told me he worked for it. He told me he got a commission for every soul he brings in. He wasn't fooling; and he wasn't apologizing; and he wasn't embarrassed.

"But the usual letter, or the usual thing people say – it will go like this: You had so much courage, and I only wish I could have that kind of courage. Then I'll say to myself, courage? I wasn't courageous. I was confused. I was stubborn, I'll say that, but out of desperation, maybe. I knew that I felt myself pulled and pulled to the church, but I was worried about *why* – about the same questions my friends were asking. I wasn't as conscious of those questions, though, as they were. When I wrote those words you just read to me [I had asked her if I might, and she said, "Yes, certainly"] I may have been 'going through the motions,' a phrase my mother would use with us: 'Don't just go through the motions' meant don't pay lip service to whatever it is you're supposed to be saying or doing, but say it loud and clear, or do it thoroughly and with all the energy you can muster. I wish I had put more effort into understanding what was happening to me at that moment, when my whole life was changing. Then I would have known more, myself, about myself; then I would have been able to give people the answers when they asked me what made me become a Catholic convert, that's what they kept calling me. I thought of myself – well, not as a Catholic convert. I thought of myself as someone who had been looking for God all those years, without really knowing it, and had now *begun* to find Him, but who had a long way to go: 'the long loneliness.' That expression 'Catholic convert' was much too final and decisive and conclusive for me; and it still is. The rain and wind and fog were still swirling around me all those years ago, more so than I dared admit to myself, and I'm not in the clear yet. Who of us is?"

In *The Long Loneliness* she emphasized the theme of drama, among others – affectation, art, trying to induce emotion, induce faith. In our conversation she emphasized her confusion, her perplexed and even desolate condition, amply reinforced by the response of her Greenwich Village friends, not to mention that of Forster. Her triumph was a thoroughly qualified one, her conversion well tempered with regrets and apprehensions.

As a sincere radical, strongly critical of the social and economic injustice she saw around her, she worried that she was entering an institution that was on the wrong side of many issues.

The scandal of businesslike priests, of collective wealth, the lack of sense of responsibility for the poor, the worker, the Negro, the Mexican, the Filipino, and even the oppression of these, and the consenting to the oppression of them by our industrialist-capitalist order – these made me feel often that priests were more like Cain than Abel. "Am I my brother's keeper?" they seemed to say in respect to the social order. There was plenty of charity but too little justice. And yet the priests were the dispensers of the Sacraments, bringing Christ to men, all enabling us to put on Christ and to achieve more nearly in the world a sense of peace and unity. "The worst enemies would be those of our own household," Christ had warned us.

In passage after passage of her autobiography she makes clear how angry she was at certain elements within the Catholic church. As we talked some of that remembered anger asserted itself yet again. She reached for a copy of *The Long Loneliness*, looked through its pages, settled on a passage, read it intently, shook her head, and said, "I still feel this way."

"What way?"

She apologized for assuming I could see the page she had been reading, then she read these words aloud:

I felt that the Church was the Church of the poor, that St. Patrick's had been built from the pennies of servant girls, that it cared for the emigrant, it established hospitals, orphanages, day nurseries, houses of the Good Shepherd, homes for the aged, but at the same time, I felt that it did not set its face against a social order which made so much charity in the present sense of the word necessary. I felt that charity was a word to choke over. Who wanted charity? And it was not just human pride but a strong sense of man's dignity and worth, and what was due to him in justice, that made me resent, rather than feel proud of so mighty a sum total of Catholic institutions.

Some twenty years after she had written those sentences she was still reading them with evident passion. When she finished doing so, she put the book down and gave a deep sigh. I was surprised by her obvious anguish as she started talking about the Catholic church, saying that it was "still not what Christ would want it to be." In response to my suggestion that no church would ever meet these standards, she said, "True," but admitted that she felt sad about the various flaws of the church and kept hoping that "Catholics all over the world will pay attention to what Jesus said and how he lived." As we circled around that never-ending problem of institutional lethargy, of organized evil, I could see the old radical fire in her. At one point she straightened herself in the chair, gave me a stern look, and said fervently,

"When I see the church taking the side of the powerful and forgetting the weak, and when I see bishops living in luxury and the poor being ignored or thrown crumbs, I know that Jesus is being insulted, as He once was, and sent to his death, as He once was. The church doesn't only belong to officials and bureaucrats; it belongs to all its people, and especially its most humble men and women and children, the ones He would have wanted to go see and help, Jesus Christ. I am embarrassed – I am *sickened* – when I see Catholics using their religion as a social ornament. Peter [Maurin] used to tell me that a good Catholic should pray for the church as if it is a terrible sinner, in bad need of lots of prayers. I remember being surprised for a second to hear him say that; he was such a *devout* Catholic. But then I realized that it was precisely *because* he was so devout that he said what he said.

"As for my mood when I converted [I had again asked what her mood had been], I think it was one of happiness, as I say in the book, but it was one of disappointment and bitterness, as those passages we've been talking about make clear. I still feel the disappointment, the bitterness. I think the life of our Lord is constantly being lived out: we are betraying Him as well as honoring Him – we in the church as well as those who are outside of it. Back then I saw so many of my friends who were out-and-out atheists doing what I knew was the Lord's work; they were trying to help the poor. Meanwhile I would see the churches, Catholic and Protestant, not lifting a finger, or hedging their bets. One dear friend of mine came up to me, and she grabbed me by the shoulders and said I wasn't being a good *Christian* by converting to Catholicism. I thought she was being anti-Catholic or in favor of some Protestant denomination, but she said no, she believed that 'all the churches are anti-Christian,' that's how she put it. You know, I couldn't get her words out of my head; for the longest time I couldn't. I guess I never have; I'll still be smiling when I hear her saying that to me, and I *do* hear her, even now, in my old age. I heard her voice in my head when I wrote these lines: 'It was an age-old battle, the war of the classes, that stirred in me when I thought of the Sacco-Vanzetti case in Boston. Where were the Catholic voices crying out for these men?'"

Pointing to a page in the book, she had read the words aloud to me.

Her conversion was a newly sanctioned continuation of her way of thinking rather than a dramatic turning away from a former viewpoint. She had no trouble reconciling the life of Jesus, the preachings of Jesus, to the ideals she had upheld years before entering the church. On the other hand, her conversion did come at a time when she had just become a mother and when she had just broken the common-law marriage which had produced the child, Tamar. She became, thereafter, the kind of person she says in her autobiography she hoped to become – "poor, chaste, and obedient." Those three words kept circling in my head as I talked with her, especially the second one, *chaste*. Why should a sensual woman, with a strong interest in men, feel that Catholicism required chastity? She never went out with men after she became a Catholic. Her energies and passions were, indeed, "converted" from a bohemian life to a comparatively austere, religious one. What did her friends think of such a change, I wondered out loud, hoping to edge toward the subject of this decisive shift in her emotional and sexual life while she was still young and attractive. She often mentioned the opinions of those friends, but only their social and political remarks – the reputation the church had "back then" for being so cozy with "principalities and powers." After a while I decided to tell her directly what I had been wondering. "For you, I think – please tell me if I'm way off base here – the conversion meant the end of your sexual life, and I have tried to understand what your reasons were."

After I apologized again for bringing up such a subject, she began,

"I am not worried about being asked personal questions of that kind; you want to know something, and I've already written a lot about it, even if much of my story can be found between the lines. I suppose a psychiatrist could make a lot out of what I wrote about entering the church, but psychiatrists make a lot out of anything we do. I can remember the very moment I wrote these words: 'I wanted to die in order to live, to put off the old man and put on Christ.' Those words had been dancing in my mind for weeks and weeks, and I had written them on a piece of paper, and then I lost it, and I have never looked so hard in my life for a piece of paper. I went from wastepaper basket to wastepaper basket, and I searched every pocket in every sweater and jacket, and I think my friends thought I was acting real strange – maybe getting senile. 'What could be on a piece of paper that's so damn important to you, lady?' one of our regulars shouted at me, and I flushed with anger, I remember. He had been drinking, and he didn't mean me harm. He was trying to be helpful, actually. And he was. I said to myself, Come on. I remembered Saint Paul: 'Not the letter, but the spirit.' I just went upstairs and sat down with another piece of paper and wrote out what I could remember of the sentence. Do you know what? An hour later that piece of paper turned up; it was in a book I had been reading – no, I don't remember which one. I compared the two sentences, and they were exactly the same, word for word. Then I wrote another sentence to explain myself, on the piece of paper I had lost: 'I loved, in other words, and like all women in love, I wanted to be united to my love.' I never lost that piece of paper, and only when the manuscript was all typed and ready to go did I throw it away.

"I think those words were my way of telling myself what my conversion meant. I had to answer a lot of questions from a lot of people back then, and I began to realize that the only right way to do that is to answer yourself – I mean, say what you have really figured out is the best explanation you can find, after all your soul-searching. To say more than what I said in *The Long Loneliness* would be to repeat myself. But I guess we all do a lot of repeating in our lives.

"Something happened to me when I was around twenty-five. I think I began to feel myself drifting toward nowhere. I had lived a full and active life, and I was glad I had met so many good people, interesting and intelligent people. But I yearned for something else than a life of parties and intense political discussions, though I still like to sit and discuss what is happening in the world: 'current events,' as they say in high school. When I fell in love with Forster I thought it was a solid love – the kind we had for a while – that I had been seeking. But I began to realize it wasn't the love between a man and a woman that I was hungry to find, even though I had enjoyed that love very much and Forster and I were as close as could be. When I became pregnant I thought it was a *child* I had been seeking, motherhood. But I realized that wasn't the answer either: I loved Forster, I was as happy as I had ever been when pregnant, and when Tamar was born I was almost delirious with joy, and I could hold and hold and hold her, and feel that with her in my arms my life's purpose had been accomplished.

"But only for so long did I feel like that, I have to admit. No, it wasn't restlessness. [I had interrupted to suggest the possibility.] For years, when people talked with me about my youth, about my life in New York before I became a Catholic, they have always brought up the subject of my loneliness and my restlessness. I am to blame for the mention of loneliness, though I didn't mean the word as it has been taken by so many people. I meant a spiritual hunger; that's what I had in mind – a loneliness that was in me, no matter how happy I was and how fulfilled in my personal life. Once I was sitting and talking with Jacques Maritain. I told him that everyone wants to understand the mind, but no one is interested in understanding the soul. People will throw around the word *soul* as if it is a nice word to use when you want to compliment a person: he has a wonderful soul. When they use the word *mind*, though, they're very serious and they become analytic, psychoanalytic. He laughed, Maritain; he said it wasn't like that in the past, and it doesn't have to be, either. He said, 'It doesn't have to be like that for you and me, if we take care.' I was grateful for what he said, especially that expression 'take care.' I thought he was telling me to watch out and not fall into a trap just because there are so many people in the trap, all so glad to be there.

"There is a psychology to the soul. Dostoievski knew that and showed us how it all works. His people, in those novels, are trying to find out why they're here in the first place, or they're *not* trying to find out. I mean, they have said *no* to God, *no* to a search for understanding of our life here: the whys we ask ourselves. I have been asking *why* all my life; when you ask why, you're alone, because you don't ask answers from other people of questions that are not answerable – by other people. If you keep asking the question, you're restless, I suppose; but not restless in the psychological sense. You are wondering why we're here and what this time we're here means. You're restless spiritually. Lots of our visitors are struggling with the same religious and philosophical questions that Jacques Maritain put to himself, and of course, dear Peter. I guess Peter was restless, also! He was always on the go, and he could be considered a lonely man. He had no family – in the usual sense of the word. But you could say that Peter had a big, wonderfully affectionate family – so many people who loved him. And he was lonely only in the sense that he missed being near God all the time. But he had a vision of God, and so he wasn't really lonely at all. He was – I think it is true of many of us – lonely only because of what he *saw, saw ahead,* the moment of that meeting, that reconciliation between the human world and the divine one. Oh, I'm getting above my height here!"

She knew she had made quite clear what she wanted me to know – that "psychology" was not the point when it came to her conversion. However, on another occasion, she did say something that opened up the subject of psychology as a legitimate field of inquiry, so far as her conversion goes. "I have to believe that everything we think and do can be used by God, can bring us closer to Him, or separate us from Him, unfortunately, and I would include the emotional problems we have." When I asked her if she wanted to get specific about those problems in connection with her own life, she demurred: "I already have – in *The Long Loneliness.*" She spoke not one word more on that score, and that familiar look of firm silence persuaded me to stop asking for further psychological reflections. Moreover, she *has* told us a great deal about her life in her autobiography, and whatever the reader would find additionally interesting in *The Eleventh Virgin* is more than hinted at in *The Long Loneliness.* Her hedonism is spelled out there, as is her burning social conscience and her willingness to be jailed in pursuit of the political and economic causes she deemed to be important. At some point, though, she began to realize that there was another cry within her. She longed for a meeting with someone, rather than anyone, and could not muffle the sound. She knew she would be lonely even when she acknowledged that cry, but she also recognized that she was not "alone," that her yearnings were ancient ones reaching back to Galilee, to the Garden, to the cry of cries, with the loudest possible echo over centuries of time.

Her loneliness, then, was existential, her restlessness the impatience and hunger of the voyager whose destination is far off. After we had sat together in silence, she added a last few words. "My conversion? My conversion was a way of saying to myself that I knew I was trying to go someplace and that I would spend the rest of my life trying to go there and try not to let myself get distracted by side trips, excursions that were not to the point."

4

The Church
Obeyed and Challenged

For over half a century, as a devoutly practicing Catholic, Dorothy Day paid intense homage to an institution some of whose practices and policies she strongly disapproved. She would never be able to forget the history of the Catholic church – its enormous failures, transgressions, and blind spots and its record of sinfulness. She would never be able to forget that, in the name of the Holy Roman Catholic Church, terrible wars had been fought, men and women had been persecuted and slaughtered, lies told, licentiousness and rampant self-indulgence pursued, and betrayals committed. It was no accident that she chose to discuss her moral outrage with respect to the church at just the point in her autobiography when she was describing her conversion and her life immediately after conversion. She married the church with her eyes wide open, her determination mixed with knowing resignation.

On the one hand, she had not the slightest doubt that at no time in its mortal ministry to mortal parishioners would the Catholic church be free of sin. One can pronounce the word of God faithfully without living in accordance with His teachings from day to day. On the other hand, she knew that we are judged not only by our mistakes, but our purposes, our intentions. She was not one of those converts for whom "sweetness and light" descend upon the entire world once baptism has taken place. Before she became a Catholic, she was forever taking herself to task and saw no reason to stop doing so after becoming one. There *is* a triumphal note in *The Long Loneliness*, but it was muted, qualified by a tough acknowledgment that the convert was still a sinner, and that the institution to which she had entrusted herself was thoroughly flawed.

In the chapter that follows the account of her conversion, she makes quite clear her strong loyalty to certain secular ideals which would be upheld by her, though constantly tested, until the end of her life. She saw her religious life as a matter between her and God – and therefore not a reason for estrangement from her many thoughtful friends in New York and elsewhere. But her own view of the Catholic church as a bastion of narrow-minded privilege was shared by a number of these friends. "After I became a Catholic I began little by little to lose track of my friends. Being a Catholic, I discovered, put a barrier between me and others; however slight, it was always felt."

Perhaps she exaggerated a little; a good number of secular friends and, ultimately, admirers[1] remained loyal – their grave doubts about Catholicism and her embrace of it notwithstanding. Still, during the first years of her Catholicism especially (and before the Catholic Worker Movement enabled her to reach out to the secular world in a compelling, convincing way), there was a good deal of what she once described as "sifting and sorting." When I asked for a bit of elaboration on that handy phrase, she declined at first. She did not want to draw up a list of people for me. Then she reconsidered – not to mention people or places, but so that she could recreate the way she felt in her early years as a Catholic, a Catholic who loved the church's sacramental life but kept finding its political and social life appalling.

She began with the devastating Romano Guardini quote "The Church is the Cross on which Christ was crucified." It clearly haunted her; I counted it in my tape scripts eleven times! When she wasn't using it directly, she called upon François Mauriac or Georges Bernanos for a similar attack from within. These two intensely loyal Catholic novelists had no illusions about the church's capacity to harbor the devil and multiply him into a legion of respected ecclesiastical functionaries.[2] When she had made her overall point, she became trenchantly particular, and I was impressed by the ability of this woman, then over seventy, to specify the particular social and historical context.

"I'm not saying things have totally changed, now, but I do believe the church in this country – and all over the world – is much more interested today in the poor, in the workers, and less the property of the wealthy and the politically influential. I remember, years ago, walking past certain Catholic churches and cringing; I didn't know whether I should start crying or scream with all my might, and I'll say it, start picketing. The sight of all that wealth – the buildings and the residences where the bishops or the priests lived. And the statements those bishops or priests made, in the church or in the Catholic press or through the many newspapers people read back in those days, before television did such a job on the American family paper.

"The cardinals here, so many of them, thought of themselves as God's favorites – as princes not of that humble, humble Jesus, but that big company of theirs. I had a Marxist friend who called the Catholic church 'a great, big, successful corporation, an international corporation,' and I never cringed when I heard him speak like that. I didn't like his bias, but I knew he was speaking the truth – a partial truth, but an important truth. Especially before Peter came along, it was a truth (I'll be honest) that haunted me every single day. I remember, after the Depression began, seeing hundreds of people on the street, begging and hungry and with a look of sadness in their faces that made me want to cry. Then I would see well-dressed people coming out of Manhattan churches, with their furs and their English-style suits and overcoats and their shoes shined and their heads lifted high: as complacent as could be in their conviction that God was *theirs* – that an hour at Mass on Sunday had put Him in their corner.

"Oh, who was *I* to criticize those people? Who was *I* to try to tell them what they should do! But I couldn't stop myself.

I got angrier and angrier at what I saw. I wanted the churches to open their doors, to let the poor and the hungry and the homeless come inside, to feed them, to give them shelter. I wanted all the gold and the furs, all the fancy jewels worn by the princes of the church, the prelates – all that to be sold, so men and women and children could get a meal and not shiver and get sick on the streets, with no place to go. When I wasn't becoming ashamed of my church, I was becoming ashamed of myself. I remember the envy I felt toward my radical atheist friends; they were fighting on behalf of the poor, and I was a Catholic and praying for the poor, and I believed it was important to keep praying, but I wanted to be out there helping in some concrete way, and I was being told in sermons that atheistic communism was the worst possible thing, and all right, I said to myself, I can understand the Church standing up to communists who wanted to destroy it – I knew *their* arrogance – but how about the church living up to its own founder's life, which wasn't the life of a Henry Ford or a J. P. Morgan? And how about *our* arrogance, the kind you can hear in church homilies, when you get the feeling the church is there to help those who have a lot to get even more by praying, while the millions of poor all over the world – including the ones living just outside the doors of so many Catholic churches – are forgotten?"

Pausing in her polemic, Dorothy Day stirred her tea to make sure all the honey was dissolved. I picked up her copy of *The Long Loneliness* opened it, and found the passage I was seeking: her account of herself as onlooker, while her old radical friends were at work organizing the march of the hungry on Washington in 1932.

On a bright sunny day the ragged horde triumphantly with banners flying, with lettered slogans mounted on sticks, paraded three thousand strong through the tree-flanked streets of Washington. I stood on the curb and watched them, joy and pride in the courage of this band of men and women mounting in my heart, and with it a bitterness that since I was now a Catholic, with fundamental philosophical differences, I could not be out there with them. I could write, I could protest, to arouse the conscience, but where was the Catholic leadership in the gathering of bands of men and women together, for the actual works of mercy that the comrades had always made part of their technique in reaching the workers?

Her envy was grounded in actuality, and would remain with her even later in life, when the church had significantly changed. Not all of it had changed, she knew, and not enough for her. "It is a constant struggle," she continued. "Jesus came to bring us 'not peace, but the sword.' He meant us to fight for those He fought for, to fight for those He chose to be with. He lived with the rejected ones, the scorned ones, and the more luxurious and important our lives, the further we are from Him, from living His life." She paused with that stern reprimand, and I sat there, gulping and fidgeting. She then asked me to read another passage from *The Long Loneliness*. She picked up the book, thumbed through the "Jobs and Journeys" chapter, and handed the book back to me, pointing at the section. "The years have passed, and most of the legislation called for by those workers is on the books now. I wonder how many realize just how much they owe the hunger marchers, who endured fast and cold, who were like the son of man, when He said, 'The foxes have holes, and the birds of the air have nests but the Son of Man hath not where to lay His head.'"

She was raising a matter that had troubled her because she fought so hard over it with her radical friends: the church as an anodyne. She explained:

"There He was, homeless. Would a church take Him in today – feed Him, clothe Him, offer Him a bed? I hope I ask myself that question on the last day of my life. I once prayed and prayed to God that He never, ever let me forget to ask that question. I told a priest about that prayer, and he got annoyed with me. He said I was setting myself up as the moral custodian of the Catholic Church. I was floored. I thought he had punctured a big bubble of pride in me. But later, I got angry, because I knew how he lived. I'm not the one to judge others – least of all a priest – but he's not the one to turn an ordinary sinner like me into such a would-be big shot: the moral custodian, indeed. I have enough trouble wondering what to do, on any day of my life, with the limited amount of time and energy the Lord has given me and the limited resources we have here for others.

"Oh, he had a point, and it hurt. I think I knew it right away. Jesus practiced what He preached; the rest of us are always being tempted to be longer on preaching than practicing. I think that priest was warning me of a great danger, of becoming sold on the sound of my voice and of becoming my own fan as a reader of my words. If the church were made up of people who weren't hypocrites and who weren't convinced that they are God's chosen personal emissaries, full of every virtue and free of every vice, then it wouldn't be the church it was meant to be, a church of sinners. You can see that I'm caught in a bind here; I want the church to be less sinful, but I know we are all sinners, and I know I'm taking a chance on becoming one of the worst sinners by denouncing so many of the other sinners around.

"I sometimes put myself through all this – intellectual gymnastics – until I am exhausted and want to go to sleep or so upset all I can do is go take a walk and hope my mind will become distracted by the sight of a nest of birds on a tree, or the ocean – if I'm on Staten Island. The ocean is especially helpful: the sight of it and the sound of it give me great reassurance, make me feel strangely at peace, even if there's all that turmoil in the sea and the noise and the waves crashing, swept by the wind, and the poor sand, meant to take all the pounding and never make a sound. When I look at the sea I know that we are meant to stop our intellect dead in its tracks every once in a while or we'll torture ourselves to death with it. Jesus didn't carry big reference books with Him, and He wasn't a college graduate. He spoke to those poor fishermen and to the sick and the poor and the people who were ostracized and thrown in jail. He spoke to them out of His heart, and with those stories and parables: all the moral energy in them. If looking out to sea doesn't completely quiet me down, or watching birds on a tree, a story of the Bible will help. I have carried my Bible to a bench in a park or sat reading the Bible on the sand, and somehow I'm not fighting with that priest any more, or with my church, which I do love, for all its failures; and God spare me for being one who keeps mentioning them."

This tension would never leave her. These feelings were particularly strong in the early 1930s, during the Depression. She was not a person who could go her own relatively comfortable way in the face of such suffering. She had become a Catholic in hopes of continuing the efforts she had made earlier as a political activist, now *sub specie aeternitatis*. Yet she felt quite alone – a practicing Catholic who had no Catholic activist friends. Before she left Washington, on the conclusion of the march of the poor to that city, she tried hard to take her case to God:

When the demonstration was over and I had finished writing my story, I went to the National Shrine at the Catholic University on the Feast of the Immaculate Conception. There I offered up a special prayer which came with tears and with anguish, that some way would open up for me to use what talents I possessed for my fellow workers, for the poor.

"As I knelt there, I realized that after three years of Catholicism my only contact with active Catholics had been through articles I had written for one of the Catholic magazines. Those contacts had been brief, casual. I still did not personally know one Catholic layman.

Her prayer was answered when, on her return to New York City, she met Peter Maurin, the Catholic layman who was to change her whole life. Peter Maurin, whom Dorothy Day has

71

described in a Catholic magazine as "a short, broad-shouldered workingman," had a weather-beaten face and "a suit that looked as though he had slept in it." He was in his mid-fifties, an animated, vibrant, passionately articulate man who captured her attention immediately and her devotion soon thereafter. It was almost as if one of the many poor and ragged and unassuming men who frequented the Depression-era streets had suddenly become possessed by God and turned into a ragged disciple.

Peter Maurin offered Dorothy Day a new respect for the possibilities within the Catholic church, for the Franciscan tradition. He offered her his own relentless insistence that the spirit of the Catholic church has to be fought for – that the fate of the Church rests in each Catholic's heart and mind and soul, in each Catholic's daily deeds. Again and again her new teacher insisted that it is foolish and sinful to accept the reality of a particular society by sitting back and railing against its great power and awesome resources, thereby abdicating one's responsibility to use one's God-given capacity for independent initiatives. Just because newspapers and politicians and rich parishioners bow and scrape before a cardinal does not mean that any Catholic who is struggling to live up to his or her religious values need do likewise.

Peter Maurin taught her to put aside some of the timid practicality, the money consciousness, the acquiescence in the face of the conventional which afflict even those who protest against society. "Among his ideas it was the one of publishing a paper which most immediately appealed to me," she recalled in *Loaves and Fishes*. She also was honest enough to tell her quick doubts: "But how can it be done without money?" Maurin's reply reveals his particular strength, a faith that had no use for such words as *impossible* or *expensive* or *unfeasible* or *unworkable*. "In the Catholic church," he declared, "one never needs any money to start a good work." In contrast to the church authorities whose pastoral letters urge parishioners to offer as much money as possible at collection time, lest important projects not be implemented, Maurin told Dorothy Day: "People are what are important. If you have the people and they are willing to give their work – that is the thing.

God is not to be outdone in generosity. The funds will come in somehow or other." In a curious turn in the autobiography, she asks, "Did he really say this? I cannot be sure now, and I suspect that he passed over my question about money – it was not needed in the Church. The important thing was work."

Peter Maurin showed Dorothy Day how to follow the lead of Jesus in the name of a church she loved, yet found terribly compromised, flawed, even betrayed outright by high-living, self-important officials. "Without him I would never have been able to find a way of working that would have satisfied my conscience." She said to me once that "Peter's arrival changed everything, everything." She added, "I finally found a purpose in my life and the teacher I needed." But the teaching fell on fertile ground. Many of the same ideals had been a force in her life. In *Loaves and Fishes* she writes,

He who is not a Socialist at twenty has no heart, and he who is a Socialist at thirty has no head," he was fond of quoting from a French author. Since I had been a Socialist in college, a Communist in the early twenties, and now a Catholic since 1927, I had a very definite point of view about poverty, unemployment, and my own vocation to try to do something about it all.

A little further in the same book she mentions the continuity between her experience and his teaching:

Peter Maurin spoke to me often of his ideas about hospitality, a concept I understand well because I had lived so long on the Lower East Side of New York – and the poor are noted for their hospitality. "There is always enough for one more," my brother's Spanish mother-in-law used to say. "Everyone just takes a little less." Poor families were always taking in other needy ones. So, when Peter began talking about what "we need," it sounded clear and logical.

Dorothy Day found other influences to support Maurin's inspired moral teaching. In her autobiography, right after mentioning

Peter's faith in a divine scheme of things that would eventually provide, she tells the reader,

> I had been reading the life of Rose Hawthorne Lathrop.[3] She was a daughter of Nathaniel Hawthorne, the nineteenth-century American novelist. Rose, with her husband, had become a convert in 1891. She had started a cancer hospital for the poor and homeless – such institutions were a rarity in those days – in three dark, airless rooms down on the East Side. Her beginnings had been as humble as ours would be if I started the work Peter wanted. Indeed, when Rose herself fell ill with grippe, her very first patient had to take care of her. But from that simple start her work had grown until there are now a half-dozen of those hospitals, run by the Dominicans, scattered around the country. A new order of nuns, wearing the Dominican habit, came into being as a result.
>
> Reading about Rose Hawthorne Lathrop and listening now to Peter so inspired me that I was quite ready to believe that in the Church no money was necessary. I was all for plunging right in. After all, I had a typewriter and a kitchen table and plenty of paper and plenty to write about. The thing was to find a printer, run off the first issue and go out on the streets and sell it. Beginnings are always exciting.

Here the American entrepreneurial spirit is put in a spiritual context. One makes do with what is available; one fashions a product, then seizes the day and goes to sell what has been made. Capitalist gusto works its way into this communitarian effort, and no hierarchical patrons are deemed necessary. New World enterprise helps make Peter Maurin's fine ideas a concrete, daily reality, as in R. H. Tawney's phrase "the Protestant Ethic and the Spirit of Capitalism."[4] On the other hand, Maurin most certainly did find precedents in Catholic history for his eager pupil, precedents for their glorious irreverence and their skepticism with respect to authority. "Obedience can be quite contagious, even infectious, even life threatening," Dorothy Day once said – and remembered saying to Maurin. But he had found the answer right in her own library.

"Perhaps he chose this method [of teaching me] because he had noticed my library, which contained a life of Saint Teresa of Avila and her writings, especially about her spiritual foundation, and a life of Saint Catherine of Siena. 'Ah, there was a saint who had an influence on her times.' he exclaimed. Then he plunged into a discussion of Saint Catherine's letters to the popes and other public figures of the fourteenth century, in which she took them to task for their failings."

Many times, as we talked, she went back to those words and tried to recapture the excitement she felt as Peter Maurin taught her the long history of Catholic dissent, the continuing struggle of one person after another to reform the church, to obey it while challenging it. She had been a citizen reformer, one who loved America enough to want to see it become a more just nation. Now, eager to become a Catholic reformer, she was keen to know the history of earlier confrontations between activists and the greedy, rich clergy who sat on various thrones the world over. She refers in this regard to "the good intellectual food" which Peter Maurin was supplying her (actually, they were feeding one another). She had been foraging for some time in the field of Catholic essays and Catholic novels; she wanted to see how the church had affected the lives of literary and political people. She also wanted to see how much freedom of mind was permissible for those in an institution with a reputation for dogma, for insisting on its special authority and its "infallibility."

This independence of spirit toward church authority remained with Dorothy Day in later life. In *Loaves and Fishes*, written in 1963 and meant to be "the story of *The Catholic Worker*," she says about the Catholic church, "It was founded upon Saint Peter, that rock, who yet thrice denied his Master on the eve of His crucifixion. And Jesus compared the Church to a net cast into the sea and hauled in, filled with fishes, both good and bad. 'Including,' one of my non-Catholic friends used to say, 'some blowfish and quite a few sharks.'"

That last quotation was the kind one heard from her occasionally. She had a delightfully wry sense of humor and could smell false piety quickly. Ten years after she wrote *Loaves and Fishes* I heard her speak in a similar vein.

"There are days when I want to stop all those poor people, giving their coins to the church, and tell them to march on the offices of the archdiocese – tell all the people inside those offices to move out of their plush rooms and share the lives of the hungry and the hurt. Would Jesus sit in some big, fancy, air-conditioned room near the banks and the department stores where the rich store their millions and spend their millions? Would He let Himself be driven in big black limousines, while thousands and thousands of people who believe in Him and His church are at the edge of starvation? Would he tolerate big mansions and fancy estates and luxurious traveling, while people come to church barefooted and ragged and hungry and sick, children all over the world? In my mind, there is only one answer to questions like those: no!

"I'm afraid that going to church puts many of us to sleep. We become so pleased with ourselves – our virtue, for attending Mass – that we forget about how others are living, who don't have the kind of lives we have. Another of my non-Catholic friends once said to me, 'Dorothy, Jesus never went to church on Sunday, so why do Catholics?' I thought he was being foolish, and told him so. I explained the problem – the struggle Jesus had with some of the Jewish officials as well as the Roman ones. But my friend kept pushing me. 'Jesus wanted people to love others, to give of themselves to others, not to fall in love with buildings and altars and prelates and popes, and not to give their time and money and faith to all that.' I told him right, absolutely right. But he said I can't have it both ways; I can't agree with him and with what 'they' tell me in church. Well, I told him I can. I said I can go to church and pray to God, and when I pray, I can say anything I want, and He is listening, and no one else. Once I asked a priest in confession if I was being out of line by thinking thoughts like the one my friend had, while sitting there in church. He laughed, and said he was afraid too many people don't have any thoughts in church; they just go through the motions. I told him I feel like crying sometimes, or I flush with anger: to be in church isn't to be calmed down, as some people say they get when they are at Mass. I'm worked up. I'm excited by being so close to Jesus, but the closer I get, the more I worry about what He wants of us, what He would have us do before we die."

In founding *The Catholic Worker* with Peter Maurin, Dorothy Day found one such mission. For the first issue, the text was typed, then taken to a printer; he received $57 for putting out twenty-five hundred copies of what she later described as "a small eight-page sheet the size of *The Nation*." The money came from two priests, a nun, and one of the two founders. (Peter Maurin had no money at all.) Initially there was no office, no staff, no promotion, no mailing list – merely the desire of two Catholics to address their fellow human beings.

Thousands of Catholics, and non-Catholics, too, responded to *The Catholic Worker* – the newspaper and the communitarian, egalitarian, populist,[5] and Christian voice it offered to an America in deep distress. At first the church as an institution offered no real opposition to the Catholic Worker Movement, which was, after all, a lay effort on behalf of the needy. But by 1937 and 1938, with Hitler and Mussolini increasingly on the rise, Spain was torn by a vicious civil war which became a holy crusade for millions of Catholics. Franco was seen as the savior of the church, with the Loyalists as proxies for the devil itself – "Red Communist Russia," as the phrase went in those days. Dorothy Day's attitude toward the Spanish civil war earned her the strong disapproval of many Catholic readers and members of the church's hierarchy. Her editorial "On the Use of Force," which appeared in October 1938, made her position quite explicit. "We are not praying for victory for Franco," she declared. At the same time, however, she pointed out that she was not "praying for the loyalists" either; she acknowledged that some of their "leaders" are, in fact, "trying to destroy religion." Rather, the Catholic Worker family was "praying for the Spanish people – all of them our brothers in Christ, all of them Temples of the Holy Ghost, all of them members or potential members of the Mystical Body of Christ." As early as 1936, *The Catholic Worker* had solemnly warned its readers that "Catholics who look at Spain and think Fascism is a good thing because Spanish Fascists are fighting for the Church against Communist persecution should take another look at recent events in Germany to see just how much love the Catholic Church can expect."

For Dorothy Day that war was a long torment, her own loyalties achingly split.[6] She didn't have to go to Spain, as George Orwell and Simone Weil had, to learn of the insincerity and manipulative cruelty which supposedly "socialist" or "communist" groups, all full of high-minded rhetoric, were constantly showing. In her personal life she had seen leftists behave meanly and deceitfully, with no regard for anything or anyone. But she also had no illusions about Franco, no doubts as to whom he owed his allegiance: a handful of powerful landowners who cared not a whit about a backward nation's impoverished peasantry, a handful of business leaders who wanted to crush a developing labor union movement, and not least, a church all too intimate with the morally discredited nobility.

Even in the 1970s, Day found herself saddened and troubled as she recalled that war and its significance not only for Spain, but for her and her coworkers in New York and elsewhere:

> "It was one of the worst times we had. We were Catholics. (We
> *are* Catholics!) The church was on one side, and there *were*
> atrocities committed against priests and nuns. My radical
> friends – just about every one of them – were for the Loyalists.
> I could see why: the Loyalists were fighting for the working
> people, the poor, the peasants. The Franco people, the
> Nationalists, were for the royalty, the rich people – and the
> church. I didn't know the Spanish church of this century; all I
> knew was what I had read from Saint Teresa and Saint John of
> the Cross. Oh, that's not true; I knew that the Spanish church

was *not* the church of the hungry and the masses of urban workers who were trying to get a fair wage. Peter was extremely upset; we all were. We wanted the Loyalists to be Christians in their faith, in their *actions*, so that we could be wholeheartedly with them. But we knew otherwise.

"You want to know how [we knew otherwise]. Well, I'll tell you: I knew people who had gone over, who had volunteered to fight for the Republic; they were the Republicans, against the Nationalists. (Lots of people, by now, have forgotten how the two sides were called in our papers, every day.) These friends saw what Orwell saw, and Simone Weil; they saw what Bernanos saw on the other side, the Nationalist side. They came back and told us. Those friends weren't upset about what the Loyalists were doing to Church buildings, or to the clergy who preached in them. They were atheists, mostly, or if they had a religious spirit, they had – how did they put it? – other priorities. I remember one friend saying to me that he knew bad things were being done on both sides, but he knew which side was the right side, and there is always wrong on every side, he kept saying. I knew what he really meant, that he didn't care about what was happening to the Catholic church. He probably was glad that the church was under attack: it was reactionary. He would never have defended the killing of people, of nuns and priests and devout Catholics coming out of a church, but he was taking sides, and he kept saying to me, 'We've all got to do it, take sides.'

" 'No', I said; no, I kept saying to myself. Our side should be a side that follows the teachings of Jesus. We are Christians, which means we take our Lord's words and His example as the most important message in the entire world. When my friends back then kept saying that the Catholic church in Spain was fascist, was part of a fascist coalition, was corrupt and a bulwark of all the worst, most exploitative elements in Spain, I had to agree. I knew what they were saying was politically and economically true. As a matter of fact, long before the Spanish civil war started there were Catholic bishops and priests and nuns in *this* country who showed no interest in how the ordinary workingman, and the poor people live and what the church should mean to them. When my radical friends stopped me on the street and said they knew I was going to 'sign on' with the Fascists in Spain, I told them they should try to give a few of us just a little credit for being independent human beings who make our decisions for ourselves and speak for ourselves. But they always rush to say that they are convinced we can't, we Catholics, think in an independent way. We are told what to think; we have to obey or else. It is nonsense, what people can sometimes believe and say.

"We lost a lot of readers during those Spanish civil war days, and some of them, I'm sure, never became our readers again. It was all right for us to be concerned with the poor during the worst days of the Depression; it was something else to say that we weren't going to uphold a policy of anything goes when 'godless communism' is exported from Russia to Spain. I knew how terrible Stalin was, and I had no use for what the Russians were doing in Spain, any more than I had for what Hitler and Mussolini were doing. I also had no use for Franco and for plenty of the church people who adored him, in Spain and here. I shouldn't put it this way, no use. Do you see how our language tells us about our jeopardy, our moral and religious jeopardy? We appealed in *The* [*Catholic*] *Worker* for the prayers of our readers – their prayers for *all* the people fighting in that civil war and caught in the killing going on there, one massacre after another, one vendetta after the other; their prayers for all the world, which was watching that awful war and taking sides and defending one group of murderers and screaming against another group of murderers. If ever Christ was being wounded, it was then.

"I was always getting lectures from people, lots of critical ones, and there were priests and nuns who told me I had gotten lost – or worse. But we held to our position, and we got some friendly and grateful letters. And there were priests and nuns – not many, but a few – who stood by us. I still remember them, what they said. I still remember the strength they gave to us at a time when we needed any friendly smile and nod we could find."

Her relationship with Francis Cardinal Spellman of New York City became the stuff of legend during her lifetime. In 1949 the gravediggers of Calvary Cemetery in New York City went on strike against their employers, the Catholic church. The cardinal refused to negotiate with them. Ultimately the strikers gave in and returned to work. Dorothy Day sided with the gravediggers, and members of the Catholic Worker community picketed at the cemetery. In *The Catholic Worker*, she made clear her feelings, declaring that "a Cardinal, ill advised, exercised so overwhelming a show of force against a handful of poor working men. It was a temptation of the devil to that most awful of all wars, the war between the clergy and the laity."

A bit of that war may have threatened to engulf *The Catholic Worker* and the New York archdiocese in early March of 1951, when Dorothy Day was asked to come to the chancery office. There, Monsignor Edward Gaffney told her she must change the name of *The Catholic Worker* – ostensibly because the word *Catholic* implies an official church connection when such was not the case. Dorothy Day discussed the matter with her coworkers, and they refused the request. She pointed out in a letter to the monsignor that she doubted anyone "thinks the Catholic War Veterans (who also use the name Catholic) represent the point of view of the Archdiocese any more than they think *The Catholic Worker* does." She was ready to take advice and criticism, to get down on her knees and pray, to try her utmost to achieve a more humble life as a writer and editor. But she was not ready to change the name of a paper then eighteen years old, with tens of thousands of readers all over the world. The church never again pressed the issue.

What would she have done, had the church demanded her compliance? She had been much quoted as saying she would oblige, that had Cardinal Spellman asked her to stop publication, there would have been no more *Catholic Worker*.[7] I had heard her talk on that subject once or twice in the middle 1950s, and in 1972 I asked her to reflect on the serious issues at stake for a Catholic who challenges church authority. She didn't like the way I put the request, as she made clear right away.

"I didn't ever see myself as posing a challenge to church authority. I was a Catholic then, and I am one now, and I hope and pray I die one. I have not wanted to challenge the church, not on any of its doctrinal positions. I try to be loyal to the church – to its teachings, its ideals. I love the church with all my heart and soul. I never go inside a church without thanking God Almighty for giving me a home. The church *is* my home, and I don't want to be homeless. I may work with the homeless, but I have had no desire to join their ranks."

At that point she stopped, and the silence became a prolonged one. I felt compelled to end it with a question: "Then the reports have been exaggerated – of your difficulties with the cardinal, with the chancery office?" She sat still, and said nothing. Finally I decided to change the subject. I told her that I didn't want to bring up a subject she had no interest in discussing and turned to the matter of her pacifism. She smiled at last.

"Well, *that* brings us back to the cardinal! He was no pacifist, you can be sure. He was a member of the church militant. I think he'd have gladly gone off to lead a march on the Kremlin, if he only could have found others to join him. I can understand why. I think the Kremlin is what the cardinal said it was, a center of atheism and of totalitarianism and of hatred and persecution: a center of evil. Of course, we've got plenty of evil here, too. Capitalism and communism – strangely alike in ways: the callousness, the arbitrariness, the militaristic passion, justified by talk of history and of manifest destiny.

"But Cardinal Spellman couldn't order me to go to Russia with him to fight with the Russians. I have my own way of disagreeing with them. Anyway, the point is that he is our chief priest and confessor; he is our spiritual leader – of all of us who live here in New York. But he is not our ruler. He is not someone whose every word all Catholics must heed, whose every deed we must copy. I know that you already know what I am saying, but we all forget, or we don't quite remember correctly. The Catholic church *is* authoritarian in a way; it won't budge on what it believes it has been put here to protect and defend and uphold. But the church has never told its flock that they have no rights of their own, that they ought to have no beliefs or loyalties other than those of the pope or one of his cardinals. No one in the church can tell me what to think about social and political and economic questions without getting a tough speech back: please leave me alone and tend to your own acreage; I'll take care of mine.

"It is true that Cardinal Spellman had no great love for some of the things we wrote in *The Worker* or said in public. I am sure, sometimes, he became annoyed with us, or maybe he never really knew much about us and cared less. I'll never know why I was asked to go to the chancery office, and I'll admit I was nervous when I went there, just as I would have been nervous, even more so, if the cardinal had summoned me. I would have tried to oblige him in every way possible. I would have bowed to him as a great spiritual leader, an important representative of God's, of His church. But there is no way he would have ever called me to do something I didn't want to do, unless the issue was a *religious* one.

"I know very well that Cardinal Spellman didn't like *The Worker*'s politics. He wasn't the only one. Lots of Catholics were angry with us when we refused to call Franco a great defender of Western, Christian civilization. Lots of Catholics were angry at us when we maintained our pacifism, with agony, during the Second World War. Lots of Catholics were angry when we weren't running to build bomb shelters in the 1950s, when we protested the madness of bomb shelters in a nuclear age, the madness of war in *any* age. Maybe Cardinal Spellman never even heard of *The Catholic Worker*. Who am *I* to assume that he had nothing better to do than worry about us, down here in the Lower East Side? But if he did pay close attention to us, then he knew how loyal we were to his church, to our church, how loving of it. You used the word *challenge*; well, I have never wanted to challenge the church, only be part of it, obey it, and in return, receive its mercy and love, the mercy and love of Jesus."

Though I saw her point, the distinction she made, quite clearly, and accepted the sincerity of her every word, I also couldn't stop certain words – pietistic, sentimental, evasive – from crossing my wicked head in connection with her statements. I was irritated. Look, I wanted to say to her, the church has tried to muzzle lots of people, and maybe some of its powerful figures have wanted to muzzle you – and I suspect you knew they did. I'd like to know whether you had a response ready, a strategy to put those political churchmen on the spot, had they gone after you in the way they may well have contemplated.

I think she saw all those words strewn across my face. I think she realized that her shrewdness as an activist was evident, and so was her capacity to anticipate a potential political stalemate. I think she decided, finally, to put some cards on the table with a friend.

"I never believed that the monsignor who wanted us to shut down or delete the word *Catholic* from our paper was acting on his own. I'm sure at least a few monsignori were in on the act. Maybe his eminence, the cardinal. Maybe not. I think they realized that we were going to pray *very hard*, to pray and pray: in churches and in homes and even on the streets of our cities. We were ready to go to Saint Patrick's, fill up the church, stand outside it, in prayerful meditation. We were ready to take advantage of America's freedoms so that we could say what we thought and do what we believed to be the right thing to do: seek the guidance of the Almighty."

On another, later, occasion she clarified and confirmed this strategy, which she applied both in this world and beyond. I remember vividly the twinkle in her eyes as she said, "The dear cardinal had

more important people to pray for than us. Perhaps that's what
saved us – he was worrying about American patriotism and raising
lots of money for buildings, and that gave us our opening: we
caught the good Lord's ear and He saw no reason not to help us
out." Then she added, "We did pray a long time for [Cardinal]
Spellman. We prayed that we not be presumptuous in so praying,
but we kept praying. If he had ordered us closed, we might have
gone right to Saint Patrick's Cathedral and continued our praying
there, day and night, until the good Lord took us – or settled the
matter."

In the end I was no longer in any doubt of her intent, back then.
She chose to stand firm and tough, serve notice on the church's
local leaders that they had best carefully calculate the consequences
of any course of action they might have had in mind against the
Catholic Worker community. She had a Gandhi-like simplicity
about her as she made those statements, but as in Gandhi, a tough,
shrewd, knowing political sensibility was also at work.

Though Dorothy Day knew how to handle the church's earthly
representatives, she felt her inclination to criticize them not consis-
tent with the effort to be an introspective and humble Christian.

"I have been invited many times by friends to become a warrior, to
take on a cardinal, to take on many cardinals, to wage war with
the church. I always have pulled back, and then some people
write me or tell me I'm a coward. I don't know what to say to
them. I did not convert with my eyes closed. I knew the Catholic
church had plenty of sin within it. How could there *not* be sin
within a church made up of men and women? 'Pride is everywhere,' I think Bernanos once said, feeling low and disgusted,
I'm sure, about the same Catholic church he loved so much!

"When Peter Maurin was teaching me all his wonderful lessons, way back in the 1930s, I was ready to go knocking on
doors, to teach others. Then we got the paper going, and soon
people were calling me a leader, and I was the head of something they called a movement. I would be stopped on the street
and be told I should say something or do something, and even

in our community people would come up to me and ask what to say and what to think and what to do. It doesn't take long for you to become quite impressed with yourself. When we took our stand against Franco, lots of people criticized us, but even *more* worrying, frankly, in the long run, I began to realize only very slowly, were some of the people who applauded us, especially the people who applauded me the loudest. They had me becoming their Joan of Arc, fighting the Catholic church. Many were Catholic, too. They would write to me and tell me that the church had become corrupt and was fascist, and I was the one who could take it on. They would tell me all these terrible stories about Bishop So-and-so and one priest or another, and I guess they thought I was raising an army, and I'd go weeding out all the Fascists.

"Yes, there certainly were people in the church, important people, whose politics weren't mine. Now that's an understatement. But the really sad moment came when I found myself having [day]dreams like those of the people urging me to get involved in church politics. I would be sitting and reading, and my mind would wander, and I'd be thinking of how we might say something and put pressure on some Catholic official, and then I would come to; I'd say to myself, Dorothy, you are in real trouble, and the sooner you make confession, the better. When I did make confession, the priest would tell me that pride is everyone's problem and that I shouldn't be too hard on myself, because that can be a way of being prideful about one's special, sinful transgressions. I had no choice but to stop and take a sharp look inward.

"I didn't become a Catholic in order to purify the church. I knew someone, years ago, who kept telling me that if [the Catholic Workers] could purify the church, then she would convert. I thought she was teasing me when she first said that, but after a while I realized she meant what she kept saying. Finally, I told her I wasn't trying to reform the church or take sides on all the issues the church was involved with; I was trying to be a loyal servant of the church Jesus had founded. She thought I was being facetious. She reminded me that I had been critical of capitalism and America, so why not Catholicism and Rome? My answer? My answer was that I have no reason to criticize Catholicism as a religion and Rome as the place where the Vatican is located, where the pope reigns as the leader of the church and speaks for the church on its beliefs, its practices. As for Catholics all over the world, including members of the church, they are no better than lots of their worst critics, and maybe some of us Catholics are worse than our worst critics."

A firm ending to what was turning into an *apologia pro sua vita*. She had clearly been struggling for many years against her inclination to regard the Church as a special sanctuary, knowing that in such a sanctuary plenty of evil can be found. Certain instincts in her — an American populism, a disgust with show and pomp — prompted her to imagine a holy crusade to turn the church "leftward," to make it more responsive to the poor and the workers. Moreover, she had a political fighter's guile, as in "serpents and doves." But she was also so much the individualist that she never could let herself become obsessed by any institution, even the Catholic church, whether as its champion or as its critic.

In *Loaves and Fishes* she answers a question which tells a lot about where her allegiance lay:

Do we get church help from Catholic Charities? We are often asked this question. I can only say that it is not the Church or the state to which we turn when we ask for help in the appeals. Cardinal Spellman did not ask us to undertake this work, nor did the Mayor of New York. It just happened. It is the living from day to day, taking no thought for the morrow, seeing Christ in all who came to us, trying literally to follow the Gospel, that resulted in this work.

Then she adds this advice from Matthew 5:42–44: "Give to him that asketh of thee, and from him that would borrow of thee turn not away . . . Love your enemies; do good to those who hate you, pray for those who persecute and calumniate you."

Such was her way of approaching the world, of coming to terms with her church. She kept herself aloof from Cardinal Spellman and church authorities. When she says "literally follow the Gospel" she is making clear her intent to practice what others preach. In so doing, she was making a statement not only about what she holds dear, but about the morality of others. She was aware of the dangers of hectoring, of finger wagging, an occupational hazard of all reformers. And she did not forget her situation as a convert, as these remarks make clear.

"It took me some years to find my place in the church. It wasn't mine by birth or even youth. I came to it at the onset of my middle years, I guess you could say. I wasn't going to rush all over telling people what *I* thought *they* should be thinking and saying and doing. I felt like a lucky guest for a while, then at home, and then I did decide to try to be as loyal as possible to the example set by the head of the household and let that loyalty, if it was achieved, be my testimony, my critique."

When she finished saying those words she glanced at a nearby crucifix and got up to serve soup.

A Localist Politics

Toward the end of *The Long Loneliness* Dorothy Day draws an interesting comparison between her old communist friends, out on the streets of New York during the early 1930s doing their advocating and recruiting, and her new friends and colleagues:

> During the days of the depression the Communists and our Catholic Workers often collided in street demonstrations. DOWN WITH CHIANG KAI-SHEK! said one of their posters, when we were demonstrating against evictions. WORK, NOT WAGES was another picket sign, when what the Communists were demanding was more relief, unemployment insurance, and every other benefit they could get from the state.

As always with her writing, a simple story, a moment of experience remembered, evokes so many reflections. The Catholic Worker Movement, by its very name, emphasizes man and woman the working person, emphasizes the job as a moral and spiritual anchor as well as the key to one's economic and social situation. The Catholic Worker Movement has also stressed, from the start, another kind of work — the everyday work of charity. Charity in the Catholic Worker sense is a means by which some of us reach out to others, and are thereby rewarded. The description above also brings out the anti-statist side of the movement; it has always focused on particular communities of men and women and children, their needs and concerns, and the possibilities of a certain neighborhood's extended family rather than national or international politics. Let others lobby Washington, D.C., or London or Paris or Moscow or Tokyo, she is saying, while the Catholic Workers attend to the needs of people living nearby.

In her books and newspaper columns, Dorothy Day outlined the social and political tenets of the Catholic Worker agenda, as in *The Long Loneliness*:

Ours was a long-range program, looking for ownership by the workers of the means of production, the abolition of the assembly line, decentralized factories, the restoration of crafts and ownership of property. This meant, of course, an accent on the agrarian and rural aspects of our economy and a changing of emphasis from the city to the land.

She refers to the importance of "working from the bottom." Such would be the essential thrust of all Catholic Worker efforts: an intense, persisting localism, not as a step toward an eventual national effort, but itself the ultimate effort. This localism included both spiritual and political work: "The spiritual works of mercy include enlightening the ignorant, rebuking the sinner, consoling the afflicted, as well as bearing wrongs patiently, and we have always classed picket lines and the distribution of literature among these works."

This localism, she has observed, was "Christ's technique." She was always taking Jesus as seriously as possible; she was always trying to remember that He was an obscure carpenter who, in His early thirties, did not go talk with emperors and kings and important officials, but with equally obscure people, and thereby persuaded a few fishermen, a few farm people, a few ailing and hard-pressed men and women, that there was reason for them to have great hope.

Such localism has not always impressed would-be volunteers to the Catholic Worker Movement, or even some who have been a part of its struggles.[1] "Many left the work," she notes at one point, "because they could see no use in this gesture of feeding the poor, and because of their own shame." The shame to which she refers is an angry shame that such misery continues to exist. Such feelings make people want to take on the selfishness of society in a more confrontational manner, through political action, and were shared by her and by the others who stayed the course. But they kept to their overall purposes, the local efforts, despite a sense of futility, or moral embarrassment.

> Just as the Church has gone out through its missionaries into the most obscure towns and villages, we have gone too. Sometimes our contacts have been through the Church and sometimes through readers of our paper, through union organizers or those who needed to be organized.
>
> We have lived with the unemployed, the sick, the unemployables. The contrast between the worker who is organized and has his union, the fellowship of his own trade to give him strength, and those who have no organization and come in to us on a breadline is pitiable.
>
> They are stripped then, not only of all earthly goods, but of spiritual goods, their sense of human dignity. When they are forced into line at municipal lodging houses, in clinics, in our houses of hospitality, they are then the truly destitute. Over and over again in our work, many young men and women who came as volunteers have not been able to endure it and have gone away. To think that we are forced by our own lack of room, our lack of funds, to perpetuate this shame, is heartbreaking.

Those young volunteers have had other reasons to depart; they have sometimes taken issue with the philosophical heart of the movement; they have wanted to take quite another approach. Dorothy Day could understand them, for she always had to mediate between the old-fashioned political activist in herself, ready to push at centers of power with all her might, and the Christian novice who endeavored to keep her eyes fastened resolutely on those within reach.

Here are some remarks from one of my students,[2] a young man who traveled from Cambridge, Massachusetts, to the Lower East Side of Manhattan, then came back to Boston, fighting with himself; he was trying to uphold his ideals and his expectations, trying to live with his disappointments.

"I went to St. Joseph's House as if I was going to heaven itself — a silly, naive attitude, I realize now. I'd read Dorothy Day's books, but I hadn't really paid attention to what she meant; I was mesmerized by the aura of goodness she radiated through her gentle prose. I thought to myself, If you go and do the kind of work she has been doing, you might end up being ten percent as good as she is, and that would be a great improvement.

"I could be riding off into my own upper-middle-class sunrise, full of plans, and it's only because I went there and got to know those Catholic Worker people that I'm a little bit concerned about others and not just myself. They taught me to keep my mouth shut and to serve others. They taught me to be respectful of the poor, even of people I used to think of as bums, tramps, no-good folks. I found it hard; for a long time I was ready to leave and not spend my time with drunks and men so damn sick, and women so damn sick, sick in body and sick in mind. But I stuck around, and I began to know those people better and better — the people we served and the Catholic Worker people. Don't think it was easy, working with the Catholic Worker people; they can be a strange group. They don't seem to know much about what's going on, what's happening outside their world. They read the papers, yes, but they put all they've got into their small, small world of saying their prayers and preparing the soup and coffee and serving and cleaning up and getting the food for the next day. They're not sitting and getting outraged, the way I do, about something the president has said or some senator.

"I never really became a part of their community. I helped, but I kept having objections. I kept thinking, This is a nice experiment, but it doesn't really change what has *got* to be changed. I'd try to talk with them. I tried to tell them that they can feed their fifty people or even fifty times fifty, if they could swing it, and there would be millions out there who would still be in the same damn bind. Even the guy who gets a bowl of soup at St. Joseph's House – his problems are still there. What about all the poor who aren't Bowery bums and who have never heard of Dorothy Day or *The Catholic Worker* news-paper, or that nice man, Peter Maurin? What about all the people who would be starving to death if it wasn't for Social Security and the unemployment insurance laws and who would be in worse shape if it wasn't for Medicare and Medicaid? What about the people who get welfare and would be destitute without it?

"It's pretty tough to sit there in the company of those very nice Catholic Worker people and listen to them praying for God's help and telling one another that the state is not the an-swer, the state is 'the wrong instrument' one of them put it, and that only small factories and farms and little religious com-munities will work. What do they mean by 'work'? Who's de-fining the word? They think big government is indifferent to people, and they believe that charity should be from person to person. It all sounds great. But they're way removed from what's actually happening to millions and millions of people. They do know – I'm not saying they're unaware of what I'm talking about. [I had asked.] I'm just saying that the Catholic Worker Movement is impractical, and it just isn't going to make any difference at all to ninety-nine percent of this coun-try's problems. It's a movement for a handful of people who want to live certain intensely Christian lives. I have only admi-ration for them, but not for a lot of their ideas.

"Someone has to try and fight the big corporations, and someone has to push the government to try to help out the poor, and someone has to make the case for working people. It's ridiculous to turn your back on Washington, on American economic and political power, and keep talking about communitarianism. Hell, I'm for that. I'd like to see loving communities all over this country and in every country of the world. But meanwhile there's IBM and GM and GE and Boeing and North American Rockwell and Lockheed and General Dynamics, and lobbyists, tons of fat-cat lobbyists, and there are generals and admirals and defense contracts, and expenditures, billions and billions of dollars of them. Don't you think that if you're interested in the poor people of this country – of the world – you'd better pay attention to all that?

"You could argue that the Catholic Worker people have their heads way up in the clouds, and they just aren't involved in the really significant battles being waged now, battles which will determine whether the poor will get a better deal or whether they will not get anything much, only a handout now and then. I hate to be talking this way, but someone has to be in touch with hard reality and say what's actually happening and not just keep reciting words from the Bible and those novelists you people like so much."

With the "you people" he had managed to connect those of us who taught humanities courses to the pastoral Christian activities he had been observing. His candid espousal of a pragmatic politics did not surprise or annoy those in the Catholic Worker Movement with whom he conversed. Nor did Dorothy Day take offense when I showed her the typed transcription of his comments. She had heard all these objections, all these reservations before. She knew the importance of pressing the national government into concerted action. Moreover, she had always been well informed on what took place not only in the United States, but abroad. She read the newspapers carefully and listened to the radio.[3] Her friends, by and large, were informed. Even though she had abandoned the socialism and communism of her youth, she never could forget the tough materialism of those two modes of economic and political analysis; indeed, she had tried to connect the best of that radicalism – its concern for the poor, and its penetrating analysis of how the capitalist world works – to her own Christian outlook.

In a way, her sense of obligation was similar to that of the young student: to be as concrete and active and thoughtful as she knew how to be, in hopes of changing the world for the better. As she once put it, "If I were indulging myself here, feeding these lost souls to make myself feel better or in pursuit of my own little dream, I would be guilty, once more, of the worst sin possible, the sin of pride." She continued with this terse observation: "We all ought to be as effective as we can, do all we possibly can to change this world in the direction our Lord pointed to and the direction of our popes in their labor encyclicals [*De Rerum Novarum* and *Quadrigessimo Anno*]."

Although Dorothy Day lived and worked in a particular neighborhood, she traveled widely and kept reporting on what she saw. She mentions in her autobiography her friendship with Paul St. Marie, the "president of the first Ford local, a tool and die maker." He took her "around the auto plants"; he showed her "what the assembly line meant. . . . I met the men who were beaten to a pulp," she tells us, "when they tried to distribute literature at plant gates, and I saw the unemployed who had fire hoses turned on them during an icy winter when they hung around the gates of the Ford plant looking for work." The struggle of workers to unionize in the 1930s was very much on her mind.

> I picked up the papers hungrily; I read every word. I wanted to be there, with the men. I wanted them to fight Henry Ford and his private army to a victory for labor. Peter would have disbanded the whole Ford Motor Company, if he could have done so. Whenever the subject of the automobile workers and their struggle to unionize came up, Peter said it was a mistake to unionize; the workers should all quit, and try to find land and grow their own food. I agreed – but I knew the workers weren't going to do that; they were going to hold fast, I prayed, and outlast the gangsters Henry Ford had brought in from all over.
>
> Peter was always building a wonderful world in his imagination; he was a dreamer. I was a dreamer, too – but I had been on too many picket lines to forget them, and I had been with

95

the IWW, and I wanted to see those Ford factories unionized before the Lord moved in and got them closed! The Lord hasn't closed them down yet, but what's a decade or two in His time? Sometimes when people call me a "utopian," I say, no, I just have a different sense of time than many others have.

A peculiar sense of time was not the only quality that distinguished her way of thinking from that of many who respected her but regarded the Catholic Worker Movement as irrelevant or quaint. Especially during the 1930s the authority of the federal government became almost sacred to millions of people in the United States, for whom the New Deal seemed the one and only hope. Meanwhile Dorothy Day was referring to "the servile state," announcing that she liked the word *libertarian*,[4] discussing at length such ideas as "decentralized self-governing bodies" which would replace the increasingly bossy and intrusive statism of the capitalist West, as well as the openly totalitarian regimes which were appearing in various parts of the world.

In the 1930s the word *anarchism* stirred up thoughts of chaos and random violence. But for Dorothy Day anarchism meant *increased* responsibility of one person to another, of the individual to the community along with a much lessened sense of obligation to or dependence on the "distant and centralized state." The libertarian thrust of her agenda was extremely important to her. She did not want to compel others to think and act as she did. She realized full well that federal programs seemed to provide the answer to urgent problems, that in a relatively quick span of time a large sum of money can be appropriated to address a problem that seems, otherwise, intractable. She knew the power of the modern nation-state, its capacity to pull people together, its capacity to launch programs, to mobilize unparalleled resources. Her purposes were different, however, her approach directed at people's attitudes, at their moral lives, at their overall ethical purpose as human beings. She wanted to affect not just the overall problem, but people's everyday lives – their manner of living with one another.

In our conversations she acknowledged, however, the disadvantages of a *personal* kind of politics.[5]

"Many young people have come here and worked with us, and they tell us after a while that they have learned a lot and are grateful to us, but they disagree with us on various matters – our pacifism, our opposition to the death penalty, our interest in small communities, and our opposition to the coercive power of the state. You people are impractical, they tell us, nice idealists, but not headed anywhere big and important. They are right. We *are* impractical, as one of us put it, as impractical as Calvary. There is no point in trying to make us into something we are not. We are *not* another Community Fund group, anxious to help people with some bread and butter and a cup of coffee or tea. We feed the hungry, yes; we try to shelter the homeless and give them clothes, if we have some, but there is a strong faith at work; we pray. If an outsider who comes to visit doesn't pay attention to our praying and what that means, then he'll miss the whole point of things.

"We are here to bear witness to our Lord. We are here to follow His lead. We are here to celebrate Him through these works of mercy. We are here, I repeat, to follow His lead – to oppose war and the murder of our fellow human beings, to reach out to all we see and meet. We are *not* here to prove that our technique of working with the poor is useful, or to prove that we are able to be effective humanitarians. That's what one visitor told me we are, effective humanitarians. Then he added what he thought was his ultimate compliment. He told me that there's a lot that city and state and federal agencies could learn from us, that we have excellent relationships with our patrons, that we have become efficient and reach our target population quite well, and that we work with a minimum of friction and red-tape. I was supposed to be impressed and grateful.

"I don't mean to sound as *un*grateful as I just did. It is interesting, how we find a target for our frustrations. That man became one for me. I turned him into a representative of all the government bureaucrats and of all the agnostic reformers who want to get the poor off the streets and into various programs and projects funded by the Congress of the United States of America. Actually, he was a kind and sensitive man, and he wanted with all his heart to help as many needy people as possible. He had a vision, just as we do. He saw more and more laws helping more and more poor people to live more comfortable lives. Who am I to call his vision wrong? He was headed for Washington after he left us here, and I'm sure he is now working for one of the federal agencies. He told me once – joking, but he was serious, also – that if he could ever become secretary of Health, Education and Welfare, he would try to abolish poverty in America. I asked him why he wanted to do that. He recited all the statistics he knew, and they did sound awful, but I had the feeling he wasn't thinking of any particular poor person, but of all those numbers and percentages.

"I told him there were lots of numbers and percentages that I didn't know, but I was sure that when poverty is abolished in America there will still be plenty of poverty. And the question will be, What kind of poverty has one embraced: spiritual poverty, or a voluntary poverty meant to help one avoid spiritual poverty? He looked at me as if he was having trouble with my talk, and I could see why. I wasn't being as helpful to him as I might have been. I was *using* him, I later realized. After you've heard a lot of people tell you that you're part of a cute little experiment that has no real meaning for the tough *real* world out there, you begin to act a little cute yourself – as if you're in some trance that makes you useless – *or* you begin to look at your accusers with a jaundiced eye and ask yourself who in the world *they* are, and what in the world are *they* accomplishing with their various legislative victories, their big offices, and their massive appropriations."

She continued her joint assault on others and herself, one moment mocking the modern, bureaucratic, impersonal state, including its welfare agencies, the next minute taking herself to task for being too sardonic. One day she almost invited an argumentative exchange by baiting me in a friendly way. "I have the feeling that you don't go along with some of our ideas here; you should speak out and let us know." She had heard me talk with admiration of Franklin D. Roosevelt and Robert Kennedy. We talked for several hours about both of them and about American politics in general. She was exceptionally, poignantly forthright:

"I'm an American, and I think of myself as coming from what you call a working-class background. I know what Roosevelt meant to millions of American working people. You were a little boy in the thirties; I was much older, and I can't forget the despair. I was glad he was down there in Washington, and not the ones who were in the White House during the twenties. In this community we prayed for Roosevelt – of course we did – but we were also praying and thinking of what the popes had been saying for the last fifty years, and we were thinking of Jesus and what He told us when He was here, and we were trying to follow His lead.

"I don't want to sound sour about the New Deal. I remember how our factory workers and our farmers turned to Roosevelt and his programs. I saw the look on their faces when he visited them. He was their savior. The problem was – the problem is – he wasn't their savior.[6] His policies were an emergency response to a situation that threatened the country's stability. By the end of the 1930s the same problems were there, as serious as ever. Then came the war. You have a hard time with us on both scores, I know. We weren't New Dealers, and we would not go to war, many of us in the Catholic Worker Movement. Those were terribly dark and troublesome days for lots of us; we read and talked together and prayed together. It wasn't easy. We were opposed to Hitler and Mussolini with all of our hearts and minds. We had warned about fascism, what an evil it was, from the very beginning. We wanted to oppose Hitler; we did oppose him, constantly and actively, in every possible way open to us as Christians."

That last qualifying phrase stopped her, even as it was a signal to me: we were about to confront the nature of Christian pacifism. I was apprehensive; I found a pacifist response to Hitler incomprehensible. The pacifist side of the Catholic Worker tradition had always been hard for me to accept in the face of mass murder. I could understand the notion of "witness": the Catholic Workers as witnesses to a Christian way of life. Though it may never work on any large scale, it is important for all of us that they uphold these principles they regard as dear as – more dear than – life itself. But the pacifism of Dorothy Day and her fellow workers went beyond mere witness. They saw militarism, totalitarianism, fascism, and communism as the outcome of centuries of pragmatism and practicality; as the result of the state's being elevated again and again; as yet one more expression of man's heathen instincts allowed further consolidation.

"What would you do," she asked, "if an armed maniac were to attack you, your child, your mother?" She asked that question in *The Long Loneliness* because she knew how trenchantly it brings into focus so many other haunting questions. "How many times have we heard this [question]," she adds immediately, and then gives the answer: "Restrain him, of course, but not kill him. Confine him if necessary. But perfect love casts out fear and love overcomes hatred. All this sounds trite, but experience is not trite."

But who of us has perfect love to offer the world, and do we know, really, that it overcomes hatred? In the case of Jesus one notes that hatred overcame Him, overcame Perfect Love become incarnate. How far ought we go with our restraint – when the armed maniac is Hitler, and when our effort to "restrain" and "confine" would have to be done by men who would need guns and planes?

Dorothy Day kept struggling with the issue of pacifism as she wrote her autobiography, and indeed, she never stopped that struggle. "It is a matter of grief to me," she declared, "that most of those who are Catholic Workers are not pacifists, but I can see, too, how good it is that we always have this attitude represented among us." Then she adds one brief, pointed comment: "We are not living in an ivory tower." She knew the argument that a democratic and well-armed society such as America enables the Catholic Worker group to function, whereas if totalitarian nations had not been fought successfully (Germany) or held in check (the Soviet Union), the Catholic Worker Movement would have been crushed outright.[7] Her ultimate position on pacifism, and maybe on the whole modus operandi of the Catholic Worker Movement – its steadfast opposition to national governments, to the state as the decisive instrument of social and economic justice – is neither one of certainty nor of doubt, but one of bravely insistent self-scrutiny.

Can there be a just war? Can the conditions laid down by St. Thomas [with respect to such a war] ever be fulfilled? What about the morality of the use of the atom bomb? What does God want me to do? And what am I capable of doing? Can I stand against state and church? Is it pride, presumption, to think I have the spiritual capacity to use spiritual weapons in the face of the most gigantic tyranny the world has ever seen? Am I capable of enduring suffering, facing martyrdom? And alone? Again the long loneliness to be faced.

These are the questions of someone who had had every compelling reason, based on conviction, to stand apart from the institutions of society the rest of us take for granted, but who knew that there is, at some point, no standing apart. For Dorothy Day, the answers to these questions lay in everyday action. One day in 1973, we had been talking about localism, and she explained:

"We haven't figured out what we should do down to the punctuation marks. In fact, we haven't written a lot of the sentences. We are responding to a life, to Jesus and how He chose to live; we believe that choice says something, even now, to us who live so many centuries later. I think we believe that it is in our everyday lives that God judges us, not in the positions we take on issues, the statements we sign, the political parties we join, the causes we advocate. Oh, we put out a monthly newspaper –

we advocate and we criticize, we say yes and we say no, and I hope with some humility, though I know we fail all the time, because self-righteousness is no stranger to us all. But for me the heart of our work is just that, the daily pastoral responsibilities: making the soup and serving it, trying to help someone get to the hospital who otherwise might not get there, because he's confused, because she's not aware she even needs to go there. There are days when all morning has been taken up with cutting up vegetables and all afternoon has been taken up with trying to arrange for someone to see a doctor and then sitting with that person in the outpatient department of Bellevue Hospital, and then it is evening, and the one who has spent that day is tired and wonders whether life ought go on that way!

"Shouldn't we be using our college education, I hear some of our young people say, or shouldn't we be fighting the larger causes of civil rights and human rights and justice for the poor? Why, yes, of course, we should be everywhere, if it is morality in the abstract that we are talking about. But each day has only so many hours, and we must make our choices, our decisions, and that is what we have done here: decided to stay here and give our energies to this scene – to use your language – this *local* scene. Does our decision mean that we don't respect the choices others make? I hope not. There are times, believe me, when I want to walk away, just walk and walk and walk. There are times when I think back to those evenings in Greenwich Village when we all talked and talked, argued and argued, and when we planned our marches or protests, and I think I wouldn't mind a return to those evenings, even though I know that I couldn't stand five minutes of them.

"I'm not making the sense I'd like to make. During those evenings, come to think of it, I used to sit and listen, and I would often say to myself, Dorothy, people have different temperaments, and yours is not the kind that will last long in a living room, with learned talk, or in a government office or even on a picket line, no matter your desire to join those picket lines. I wanted to go and *be* with 'the people' I heard all those learned folks talking about. I'm being sarcastic, I know. I was capable of the same sin I've just criticized in others, lots of times: I talked of 'the people,' but I had no desire to go and share their world, only the desire to be their leader, to tell them what they should do and to tell the world what it should do with and for and to them. When my friends want to figure out what we mean by community, I say that community is all of us together, trying to be of help to each other, and some of us telling everyone else where to go and what to do and why."

She stopped and began to rummage through her books. She then smiled and noted the irony – that she couldn't seem to let only herself speak, that she was trying to find someone "higher," some authority, some writer of books, to help her justify the movement's practices and purposes.

"I have just told you that we've been struggling to break away from the subjugation of plain, ordinary folks to the distant power of others, their so-called leaders, and here I am calling on my own leaders, who have their own distant power. We all want to surrender ourselves to some institution, some equivalent, here and now, of the Almighty, as Dostoievski kept reminding us, especially in the Grand Inquisitor scene of *The Brothers Karamazov*. If I had to be very brief about what localism means, I would say it means a neighborliness that is both political and spiritual in nature."

I think Day wanted to continue, but found herself unable to do so. Instead, she reached for her familiar Dostoievski shelf, pulled *The Brothers Karamazov*, and with no trouble at all arrived at the Grand Inquisitor scene.[8] She had sometimes read aloud from one of her favorite books in the course of our talks, and I fully expected to hear her voice delighting in Dostoievski's moral and psychological challenge to secular mankind. I was trying to guess which paragraph she would select. But after ten or fifteen seconds of intent scanning, she closed the book sharply. She put it back on the shelf immediately, looked at the entire shelf, then turned to the window. Rain was pouring down noisily.

Until then I had not heard the rain at all, but now I began to resent it as an unwelcome rival. She seemed all too interested in listening to it, commenting upon its persistence. I thought her mind was "wandering" because of the difficulty of the subject at hand. She pointed out the burden rain put on the homeless or on people who already feel grim or sad. She told me of her own delight in rainy weather and her awareness of being lucky to be able to afford such a feeling. She accounted for it by going back to her childhood, to the cozy time she and her brothers and sister had with their mother, who often baked cookies during rainy afternoons. She reminded me (and herself, yet again) that others have no such memories.

Dorothy Day seemed to sense that I was about to change the subject or end our meeting for the day, because she began to bring her observations into focus, mentioning the rain in Georges Bernanos's novel *The Diary of a Country Priest*.[9]

"I always think of the priest, that wonderful curé, enduring rain. The town where he lived was an obscure one, and I remember the opening paragraphs, those words, 'Mine is a parish like all the rest.' Then, I remember the priest [in his diary] saying the parish was full of boredom, and then he describes the weather, the rain pouring, and how it gets sucked in the breath, the lungs. It was 'a desolate November day,' I think the words were, to that effect. Maybe it's *my* reading, and no one else's, but I think of the rainy, melancholy weather as an accompaniment to the curé's life, to his daily duties. Others make clear weather for themselves! They write and talk and imagine themselves getting rid of every problem, solving all the puzzles; they tell others what will be ahead, a bright, sunny future, if only they pay attention, listen to every word spoken, read every word written. Not that curé; he knew that even the best weather is only temporary, that clouds and a downpour are around every corner. But he chose to stay there, do what he could; the true reality, as our Lord told us when He chose a ministry, rather than books to write and an empire to lead.

"You ask about localism, Why localism? I think my answer is that for some of us anything else is extravagant; it's unreal; it's not a life we want to live. There are plenty of others who want that life, living in corridors of power, influence, money, making big decisions that affect big numbers of people. We don't have to follow those people, though; they have more would-be servants – slaves, I sometimes think – than they know what to do with. Isn't there just a small space in our world, our culture, for men and women who want to follow the lead of that curé of Bernanos's, and of the Lord – the one Bernanos believed to be inspiring the curé, and him, too, as he wrote that story? It has meant so much to so many of us here in this community."

The imagery worked for her, one could see by the newly quiet look on her face – not so tightly drawn. She paused, took a sustained draft of dark tea. I was hesitant to continue *talking* about localism, about a localist politics, because I thought the very discussion would be ironic, a reminder of what often endangers such a localism: too many ideas, which tempt the one who holds them to make a full-time career of talking in Washington, D.C., say, or in the media. Day had been thinking in much the same way, I would learn, but she also wanted to continue our conversation. She mentioned Simone Weil, whose *Need for Roots* she regarded as seminal and suggestive.[10] She reminded me how critically Weil treated the modern centralized state and the large corporations which are, in their own way, sprawling "states." She agreed with Weil that what gets lost under such circumstances is the ordinary person's sense of control over the everyday workings of his or her life. This is not the "alienation" Marx wrote about; it won't be solved, Dorothy Day, with a thin smile on her face, pointed out, through an advanced capitalism that gives way to a dictatorship of the proletariat, to huge state-owned factory and farm complexes. What gets lost is the personal authority of particular individuals and the authority of the family, that rock-bottom "organization" which constantly requires both ideological and practical defending these days.

We then discussed how Simone Weil could help us go from the inviting but imprecise talk of community to a specific consideration of what might characterize a local politics. We both remembered the uncanny mix of conservative and radical thinking in *The Need for Roots* – its emphasis on the importance of national traditions and customs, its support for a framework of institutions to which a country's citizens could feel attached.[11] Dorothy Day would have liked to see the church among the institutions advocated by Simone Weil to link people together: "Oh, I wish she'd been able to enjoy the [Catholic] church. God gave us the church as well as Himself; I mean He lives through it." But Simone Weil's mysticism bypassed the church; in fact she never even allowed herself to be baptized.

Like Dorothy Day, Simone Weil also recognized the idolatrous side of nationalism and its capacity to replace religious belief as the reigning secular faith, as an "equivalent of the Almighty." She also feared the authority of giant industrial companies over their workers, under which employees became peons, if not outright slaves. The time Simone Weil spent as a factory worker had confirmed what otherwise would have been an intellectual's hunch: the loss of personal authority so many assembly line workers feel and their bitter sense of anonymity and dispensability.

On the other hand, Dorothy Day and I were talking in the early 1970s, and she was quick to acknowledge that the 1930s capitalism Simone Weil had observed firsthand, in the worst years of the Depression, had been replaced by a capitalism far less harsh and demeaning for most workers. Still, she insisted that in certain respects Simone Weil's critique in *The Need for Roots* very much continues to apply. Weil saw that people wanted to feel connected to one another. She saw the modern state, capitalist or socialist or fascist, as eradicating the communal ties that people urgently crave and require. She believed that the dignity of individuals would be affirmed by local associations, by participation in meetings in which people can affirm one another face to face. Simone Weil argued for small, lively associations of neighborhoods, for the revival of the ancient meaning of the *polis*: villages, provinces, and regions which would have a continuing place in the minds of men, women, and children, and contribute to a lively civic life. Instead of a vote now and then or a big speech and banner headlines, she envisioned daily ties, actively forged and strengthened by families involved with families, workers with workers, that would add up to a people's rootedness.

Dorothy Day did not see these ideas as utopian. All of us, she maintained, had what she called

"the responsibility to hope, to dream. . . . The imagination is part of our lives – part of reality. People always question us on our realism. Oh, if we had a dollar for every comment we've received about our unrealistic attitudes, about our pacifism and our anarchist views. We are *not* anarchists in the negative sense of that word. We have our own routines and rituals. We obey the law all the time, pay our bills and try to be good citizens. A good citizen uses the Bill of Rights, says what he believes to be true, and shares his thoughts with others. A good citizen *takes part in a democracy*, doesn't leave it to others – some big-shots – to speak for him, to act for him.

"We don't happen to believe that Washington, D.C., is the moral capital of America. The people who contribute money to us don't get a tax credit, because we don't register with the government as a nonprofit, tax-deductible organization, or whatever. We hope God is keeping a sharp eye on us and will let us know quickly of our mistakes; we're less impressed with the kind of surveillance Washington, D.C., does. But we're doing our job as American citizens: we try to keep *our* eyes glued on Washington and tell our readers what we think the government is doing and why it is behaving the way it is.

"If you want to know the kind of politics we seek, you can go to your history books and read about the early years of this country. We would like to see more small communities organizing themselves, people talking with people, people *caring* for people, people coming together in order to make known what they believe and what they would like their nation to do. Apathy, like sloth, is a sin. Why do we have to think that a shrug of the shoulder is being realistic, that indifference to the bureaucratic power of federal officials, or the power of some of those union officials who behave like the company folks they bargain with is the only sane alternative?

"I know, I'm asking a rhetorical question. We believe we are doing what our Founding Fathers came here to do, to worship God in the communities they settled. They were farmers. They were craftspeople. They took care of each other. They prayed to God, and they thanked Him for showing them the way – to America! A lot of people ask me about the influences on our [Catholic] Worker movement, and they are right to mention the French and the Russian and English writers, the philosophers and novelists. But some of us are just plain Americans whose ancestors were working people and who belonged to small-town or rural communities or neighborhoods in cities. We saw more and more of that community spirit disappear, and we mourned its passing, and here we are, trying to find it again, for ourselves and for any others who happen to come our way."

She had delivered a bit of a speech, if not a sermon. She started to talk in a more personal vein, remembering people in her child-hood, children she had known when she was a child herself, friends of her parents, her brothers, her sister. She remembered a grocer who let her come and fetch things for her mother. Somehow he kept records, but she had never bothered to figure out how he did so. The point was that he knew her, knew her parents; he trusted her, trusted everyone who came to shop at his store. She could still recall in her seventies a certain "variety" store – the candy, the huge pickles, the cheese, the games, and of course, the newspap-ers and magazines. She and her friends came and went – kings and queens in the eyes of the couple who owned the store. Why? The answer was not hard to fathom: the children belonged to families who knew one another, all of whom were familiar to the family who owned and ran the store. The network of acquaintance was strong and gave the boys and girls growing up there the sense of a world fairly well circumscribed, of being easily recognized by all sorts of others.

"It is strange, to live in a world of so many strangers," she once said, as we were yet again grappling with the matter of localism in an afternoon talk. Her politics, she said animatedly, was a matter of "pursuing a community life, a community life which would be loyal to the teaching in the Sermon on the Mount." She went on to say that if more and more such communities were to form, a local politics would be at work and would affect the quality of more and more lives, and, she prayed, the nation as a whole. True, she was dreaming; she well knew that the communities she spoke of so fondly were a mere handful. Nevertheless, entire empires had been toppled by a handful of dissenters, men and women who seem to have no influence and power and no interest in obtaining them. What they have done, she reminded me, is bear witness, stand fast, huddle together in faith, in community: the early followers of Jesus, for example.

For Dorothy Day, just yesterday was when Jesus walked Galilee, and not far away will be the moment He decides to call us all to Him. To me such talk was her way of conveying her mystical faith, her sense of nearness to God. But when I asked her about this, she made clear that I had not understood.

"We are communities in time and in a place, I know, but we are communities in faith as well – and sometimes time can stop shadowing us. Our lives are touched by those who lived centuries ago, and we hope that our lives will mean something to people who won't be alive until centuries from now. It's a great 'chain of being,' someone once told me, and I think our job is to do the best we can to hold up our small segment of the chain. That's one kind of localism, I guess, and one kind of politics – doing your utmost to keep that chain connected, unbroken. Our arms are linked – we try to be neighbors of His, and to speak up for his principles. That's a lifetime's job."

Living in a House
of Hospitality

Nothing mattered more to Dorothy Day than the way she lived her life. She was interested in books and ideas, but for her the test of a life is its everyday moral texture – what one does, finally, with all the hours of each day. Of her own free will she chose a kind of life that is not the easiest to contemplate for those who come from a comfortable, well-educated, middle-class background.

For almost a half century she chose to live alongside the urban poor. She and her fellow Catholic Workers are not the kind of reformers who live in one world while hoping to change another. The Catholic Worker houses of hospitality are meant to be communities in which the so-called helpers merge with those who, in the conventional sense, would be regarded as needing help.[1] During stays in these houses, I've felt that the aim is for the workers and the guests to be indistinguishable.

In 1939 Dorothy Day published a book called *House of Hospitality*; in it she describes those early years of her Catholic Worker life – living close to people in dire straits. "Homes had to be found for the men – some had been sleeping in Central Park," she tells us in the foreword. So they rented "an eight-dollar-a-month apartment near Tompkins Square, a rat-ridden place, heatless and filthy, abandoned even by slum dwellers." But one place was not enough. "People were being evicted on all sides. We had to find other apartments, help get relief checks for them, borrow pushcarts and move them." There were homeless women, too, so "the need to start a hospice" for them also "made itself felt." She uses that passive construction, but it was her own tireless activity that got so much going at that time. "Neighbors came in needing clothes and we had to go to friends and readers begging for them" she remembered. "We cooked, cleaned, wrote, went out on demonstrations to distribute literature, got out mimeographed leaflets, answered a tremendous correspondence, entertained callers."

Every time I questioned her on how those many Catholic Worker hospitality houses got going, she described the widespread poverty of the early 1930s, and then observed, "Peter and I saw those people standing at corners, or sitting on park benches, and we felt that something *had* to be done, and right away. We never expected to solve the *nation's* problems, but we thought we ought to try to do all that we could do, and we thought that if more and more of us tried harder and harder – well, a step would have been taken, and that's what I think the Lord wants from us, as many steps as we can manage."

She managed to make many "steps."

"Throughout the country there are twenty-three hospices, each one now accommodating anywhere from a few people to one hundred and fifty. There are 'cells' made up of interested readers who are personally practicing voluntary poverty and the works of mercy. There are breadlines run at many of the houses so that now about five thousand a day are fed. In New York City over a thousand come every morning to breakfast. We have fed workers during strikes. We have been out on picket lines. We have spoken at meetings all over the country to workers, unemployed, unorganized and organized, to students, professors, seminarians, priests, and lay people."

She was always trying to reach others, to encourage them to do a stint of work on behalf of the needy. In *House of Hospitality* she tells of "thousands," men and women all over the country, who became involved as Catholic Workers. Not all of them, of course, made that most serious commitment of living for a while in one of the houses. Many came, were touched, and went back to campus or job, but with a determination to help in their own way. Some offered to do volunteer work, to prepare or serve food, to distribute clothes. Some got closer and became day-to-day members of a Catholic Worker community: a life immersed in service, prayer, and reflection.

In 1954, when she was fifty-seven years old and still a very active person, Dorothy Day told me in a letter that she "could well understand" my "reluctance to share" such a continuing life. I had visited, spoken with her, and then written her, feeling apologetic that I could not leave my medical studies to work with her. "The houses of hospitality we have going now," she pointed out in her written reply, "are meant to be of help to some people — we who live in them, and others who come to visit us, and eat with us, and pray with us; they are not meant to be a reason for anyone to feel 'inadequate' or 'selfish.'"

Her response to such *apologias* could be cogent and edifying, as I learned again in 1971, now with a machine going to record the words spoken at St. Joseph's House on the Lower East Side.

"If we are the reason for others to feel unhappy and misunderstood and wrongly accused, then we are caught in sin ourselves. It is important for us to make clear what we're doing; it is important that we not tell the world to follow us or tell the world that our way is the way to go, to be. I always want to talk with students who come here, especially the ones who come and tell me that they wish they could stay here, and they'd love to work here, but they don't have the courage, they'll say, or the strength of character, or they're too selfish — I keep hearing that word. It is not selfish to realize that this kind of living — here at St. Joseph's House or up at Haley House [in Boston] — is not for everyone. There are times, believe me, when I would include myself as someone who doesn't belong here. I get tired or I get into trouble with someone; there is tension, and even a long prayer doesn't make the tension go away.

When the outsider comes, all seems serene or noisy, but part of a decent, charitable effort on our part. The students or the teachers – we've had lots of college professors come visit over the years – are impressed. They see us feeding people who look poor and even quite sick. We are patient with those people when they scream at us, and even swear at us and the visitors think, Such angels, those Catholic Workers!

"And I'll say this: it may be that when we're watched, visited, we are tempted to be a bit angelic. We smile even more and speak even softer, not out of dishonesty or hypocrisy, I truly pray, but because we are aware that we are being observed and that we have an obligation to our visitors, even as we have an obligation to the people whom we serve at lunchtime. When we talk with our visitors we try to be as open and honest as we can be, though. I have sat downstairs for hours with friendly people, who tell us how wonderful we are; and I don't tell them they're wrong: it would be rude to say so. Anyway, it's not a matter of right or wrong, of devils or saints – and we've been called both lots of times. The real issue is what we are trying to do here. Do we understand our intentions well enough to be able to explain them to others? That is an important question for us. We are all supposed to be teachers to each other. Peter was a teacher more than he was anything else, except, possibly, an eager servant of Jesus. He was constantly teaching in those 'easy essays' of his. He taught me to be a teacher – in fact, he got a bit impatient with me at times, when he saw me hurrying around, trying to get food for our people to eat, or clothes, and not paying enough attention (he thought) to someone who had come to ask us about *The Catholic Worker* or ask us about our goals here, where we live. 'You must be as clear as you can; you must help them know what we are trying to do,' he'd say. He always reminded me that we are doing our best to spread the Gospel, as well as to do those works of charity which have meant so much to all of us.

"Did you hear what I just said? When I used that phrase 'meant so much to all of us,' I was talking about the satisfactions of the server. But satisfaction can turn into satiety. A person can start out aiming to be righteous and end up self-righteous; we can become so earnestly the doers of works of charity that we think the Lord has given us a special blessing. We walk around quite pleased with ourselves. The sin of pride."[2]

Dorothy Day was constantly struggling with this problem, with the realization that an attempt to reach others can turn into self-centeredness and self-importance. She also saw danger in the work: the failure to recognize the demonic side of one's charitable actions:

"I have had to stop myself sometimes. I have found myself rushing from one person to another — soup bowls and more soup bowls, plates of bread and more plates of bread, with the gratitude of the hungry becoming a loud din in my ears. The hunger of my ears can be as severe as someone else's stomach hunger: the joy of hearing those expressions of gratitude. I remember a nun who came to visit us. We sat and drank coffee after she had helped us work. She was a fast one. She went from table to table, arranging chairs and helping some of the men who really needed help. She was tactful and modest, and of course, they took to her. She knew who could go fend for himself and who needed a little boost from her. As we sat and talked she said to me in a whisper, 'This is dangerous work.' I'll remember her words until my dying day.

"At first I couldn't understand her, she could see. I smiled, but I guess she saw the blankness in my eyes. She kept speaking in a whisper. 'It's a grave temptation — to want to help people.' I still didn't understand what she was getting at. I was afraid she might be preparing a political lecture for me, the kind we've gotten for years from Catholics and non-Catholics, the kind that tells us we're radicals and we're Communists. I guess I had jumped ahead to what I thought her punch line would be, that the temptation was to fall into some communist trap. I was silent, though. She must have seen that the blankness hadn't lifted, so she explained herself. Still whispering, she confessed to me, 'I think God knows when I help myself by helping others. I suppose there's no way to escape that trap but prayer to Him: admit the sin and try to reserve a laugh or two for yourself, to laugh *at* yourself.' She didn't stop there. I'm paraphrasing her, but the message was clear and pointed – that we run the risk of thinking we're God's gift to humanity, those of us who struggle in our soup kitchens and hospitality houses to be loyal to Him. It is a message I hope none of us forgets, though we do; all the time we do."

In *The Long Loneliness* she mentions how arrogant and impatient she and others were when they were young and all taken up with political or social radicalism. Later, when writing in her autobiography about her early Catholic Worker days, she mentions the discussions among those who were trying to live up to such high ideals. Indeed, she makes quite clear that she and Peter Maurin not only had discussions but conflicts – strong disagreements as to what ought to be said or left unsaid, done or not done. She was, for instance, much more unyielding in her pacifism, less inclined to be silent about it during the Second World War, when almost everyone of her political background was ready to fight to the finish against Hitler. Then there were the ostensibly small failures, which she describes in stories such as this one in *The Long Loneliness*: "Once when I looked out the farmhouse window during an especially crowded time and saw some footsore travelers coming along the road and sighed, 'I suppose they are coming here,' one young worker said severely, 'You should not write the things you do unless you mean them.' In other words – do not write about hospitality unless we are willing to assume the obligations such writings bring with it."

In *Loaves and Fishes* she is even more explicit; she refers to times of discouragement. "It takes some time to calm one's heart," she adds, and then tells what has got that heart going: it is filled "all too easily with irritation, resentment, and anger." At another point in the book she makes this declaration: "How often we have failed in love, how often we have been brusque, cold, and indifferent.

'Roger takes care of the clothes; you'll have to come back at ten o'clock.' Or 'Just sit in the library and wait.' 'Wait your turn; I'm busy.' So it often goes."

All during those many years she and her daughter spent their lives in hospitality houses, among people – helpers and the helped – who could try her dedication sorely.[3] She mentions her "faults" and acknowledges her lapses: "How often I have failed in love." She acknowledges her "interior fear and harshness," her tendency to be coldly, nervously, apprehensively moralistic. On the other hand, she was wary of paralyzing self-criticism, which can be an oblique way of drawing attention to one's virtue: Look how eagerly I seek out and announce my failures. What she sought was an honorable mean, a tradition in which men and women did the necessary work, while keeping an eye out for their wayward inclinations.

She could be sharply explicit about the devilish side of herself and her companions. She never gave Satan the mighty authority some writers have, but she knew there was an unavoidable struggle between good and evil even in those who have come to believe in the saving grace of Jesus. At times, as she talked about her life, she seemed engrossed with *His* life, so that a listener felt her passion responding to the Gospels.

"I don't only think of the Passion as the Crucifixion. I think of His whole life as 'the Passion.' I don't mean to become a theologian now; I have never been good at theology. My mind isn't abstract enough. But when I think of Jesus I think of some-one who was *constantly* passionate; I think of all His experiences as part of His Passion: the stories He told, the miracles He performed, the sermons He delivered, the suffering He endured, the death He experienced. His whole life was a Passion – the energy, the love, the attention He gave to so many people, to friends and enemies alike.

"When young people come here and want to help out, they ask me all sorts of questions, and I try to answer them. I try hard to be open and honest. Sometimes I don't succeed. The devil wins. I tell our visitors about the help we offer, but I omit any mention of our troubles here. Why should I tell them our troubles, I ask myself. And I ask the question in a way that there is an answer I expect to hear: you shouldn't tell them our troubles, because everyone has troubles, and all people working together have them, and so it goes. But I know it won't do, to give the impression we sail along here, on a sea of benevolence. The students are truly hurt if we aren't willing to tell them enough to help them get through some of the devastating experiences they have when they spend time helping us do our work. Our 'guests' can be rude and mean and nasty; they can say the worst things – foul-mouthed talk. Imagine being a student who encounters such behavior and who has talked with Dorothy Day or someone else, and believes that all those Catholic Workers are able to be insulted with complete equanimity. We have lost our tempers, but for that the Lord can smile and forgive us. I'm not sure He will forgive us if we try to picture ourselves as having no tempers, as being gentle and kind, always, to everyone. The Lord Himself lost His temper a bit, and I try to remember that every once in a while. When I forget *His* humanity, I forget my own, too, and then I'm in the devil's hands. It is a temptation we have to watch for all our lives – posing."

The use of the word took me by surprise. I looked up from my notepaper and put my pen down, as if I dare not write such a word. (I had also been taking notes on what she said, while taping our dialogue.) She saw my anxious look. She looked right at me, and I found myself averting those wide eyes, those glasses which made her gaze seem all the more penetrating. She didn't break the silence, though. Finally I asked, "Do you mean to use that word – posing?" She smiled, as if to reassure me that she was not feeling patronized, and to let me know that she understood my apprehensions, without in any way feeling threatened by them.

She paused before answering my question, then took me in hand, so to speak, with a rather extended statement:

"We must respect ourselves, and so you are right to ask about that word. Oh, dear Lord, I would never want to turn us into a bunch of actors and actresses, not in my thoughts and not in what I say. But we've gladly called ourselves fools for Christ, and we might as well admit that there is drama in using that description! Saint Paul had a dramatic conversion! He was a powerful letter writer; he knew how to startle his readers! From the beginning we had to go into the street and call attention to our newspaper. When Peter heard our communist competitors shouting 'Read the *Daily Worker*,' he started shouting, 'Read the *Catholic Worker*, daily.' I think I tell that story in *The Long Loneliness*. [She does.] There was lots of drama in our lives then, at the start and afterward. We picketed. We said no when others were saying yes to Franco. We went to jail because we thought building air-raid shelters in the event of a nuclear war — well, was crazy and immoral both. I'm simplifying our positions, but we were prepared to let the world know in very bold ways what we believed.

" 'Will you people please stop *exhibiting* yourselves,' one lady came up to me and said once, when we were walking up and down the street with our signs, and I said I was sorry we were of trouble to her, but we had to keep doing what we believed to be right. We believed we should tell others what we thought and why. It is risky to preach to others. You can become a loud-mouthed bother to everyone who hears you. The preacher becomes preachy. You can become overly dramatic, too. I've worried about our people, about myself; I've worried about being disrespectful to those who don't see the world as we do. On the other hand, we have our own faith to uphold, and we have a message to bring to others. To pose can mean to become fake performers, a risk you take when you start talking to others, when you try to catch their attention. We did not choose to go into the desert and pray for all the world's people, pray and pray and pray. We've tried to pray, but we've been journalists and political activists — Christians living in the midst of a busy urban world, with people everywhere near us. No desert here, other than the vast desert of lost souls you can see on some streets.

"I have been upset with myself on certain days; I wish I could just stay in my room and pray and read and ask God for His forgiveness. I know that when I go downstairs and talk to all the people there and when I meet a lot of the people who come to visit us and when I meet some of the people we serve – well (you may be offended if I say this), I might end up posing more than I would ever want to admit to myself at the time. It's only later that we stop and think about what we've been doing and how we might do better. Sometimes later is just a few hours afterward; sometimes later is weeks or months afterward, when everything has begun to blur, but there's a thorn inside you, and it won't stop giving you discomfort until you come clean. Peter used to say to me, 'We can't expect to run to meet the world with our message and not fall flat on our faces. We've got to take the risk. We've got to get up after we fall and keep moving. If we say no, no more moving, because we made a mistake, made ten mistakes, a hundred, we're all washed up.' And we must not be all washed up, he kept saying. (He liked that expression.) I would argue with him. I would tell him that if you keep stumbling and falling, it might be because you're doing something wrong. 'Pray to God; ask for His help,' he would answer. But then he'd add, 'Keep moving, though.' I guess we have."

As she quoted from her friend, she did so with considerable dramatic intensity, and I began, at last, to understand what she had been trying to tell me: that there *was* a performing aspect to the life she lived within the hospitality houses and on the streets and in the course of her lecturing journeys across the country. Peter Maurin and she had recognized each other not only as fellow Catholics and fellow radical egalitarians in the early Christian sense, but as Pauline evangelists, eager to urge the virtues of their kind of Biblical communitarianism upon as many people as the written or spoken word could reach. His "Easy Essays" were at once comic and tragic statements, not immune from melodrama. Her essays and books took risks with sentiment and at times were unabashedly stirring. She wrote stories full of sudden turns of fate, memorable surprises, entrances and exits of friends or acquaintances: a spectacle unfolding, as in Saint Paul's phrase "for we are made a spectacle unto the world," which appears in the first Epistle to the Corinthians, as does the phrase "fools for Christ's sake."

The Bible was her constant companion in the course of the decades she spent living in hospitality houses.[4] While a list of her daily tasks would seem to cover every moment of the day – people fed, clothed, sheltered; essays written; the newspaper published; discussions; trips to the hospital, visits with the sick at home; an expression of solidarity with one or another support for activists – she also carried on another intense daily activity, reading the Bible. The Bible was for her *the* book, and when she read it she was not "just reading," as she emphasized several times when I asked her how she spent her days.

"Years ago I was much more active than I am now, as you would expect. I used to pitch in, try to do everything: not just writing for the paper, but setting it up and helping to mail it. We did it as a family. I used to help with the cooking and the serving of meals. I would go begging for the food [from wholesale and retail grocers] and the clothes, and I'd try to help keep our quarters clean and hospitable. Of course, we had our prayers, and we tried to find just a little time for ourselves.

"When people ask me about living in a community, in one of our hospitality houses, they seem to delight in hearing about all the work we do – the more the better, so long as *they* aren't doing it all. I get tired reciting our responsibilities, and I get tired hearing people say how *wonderful* it is, what we do. Lots of the time it's not as wonderful as they think. We are overworked or feel tired and irritable, and we have heard some rude remark from someone in the line [waiting to be fed] and our patience is exhausted and we're ready to explode. Do we? [I had asked.] No, not usually. I mean, not directly. We explode by being tight-lipped and looking sullen and feeling hopeless, completely hopeless about the people we're meeting.

"I remember times when I kept holding on to my rosary beads; when I prayed as hard as I could; when I talked to myself, pleaded with myself, to be more understanding of the people who come to us. There are times when nothing seems to work, though, when the energy and conviction seem to have fled, gone elsewhere. I would find myself in tears, but wouldn't know why the tears were there. 'Your eyes are watering,' I would hear, and I would say yes, they are. I have a bad cold. I guess I did. I guess I was shivering because the world seemed so bleak for all these poor folks, and I had begun to see things from their point of view. When I caught myself thinking it was a terrible shame that our guests weren't doing as I was – seeing the world through *our* point of view, *my* point of view – I began to realize that I was in real trouble. I'd pick up the Bible and read and read, sometimes spend hours on one page, going over and over a passage. The sin of pride, I keep repeating to myself, is the worst of all sins, and it lurks around every corner. We have as many corners here, I had better admit, as you do up there, where you work."

After that pointed remark, she seemed to want to stop for a while. She shook her head, lost for a few seconds in memories, ones which I guessed were unpleasant. I felt awkward, like one of those annoying admirers to whom she had just made reference. I suggested that I leave. Lunch was starting downstairs, and I would join the line of supplicants. She laughed and said she would, too. She apologized for being distracted by her thoughts, which she then described as pleasant ones. I was surprised, but didn't know how to tell her that I had thought her mood to be quite different. She saved me from saying a word, however, by starting to talk again.

"I was thinking back to some of the really wild and crazy times we all lived through. Oh, we've had some very troubled people here, some men and women who have been – as we say it – 'way out in left field.' I'm sure you would have had the proper psychiatric names to apply to them, if you would have been there. Some were dangerous. They came armed. They had knives and guns. They had been drinking a lot. They were agitated and noisy, so noisy, they quieted everyone else down. In a strange way, they could be a relief. They made all the others so frightened, so *respectful*, that they stopped *their* noise, the everyday loud talking that made such a commotion for our ears.

"I was recalling the time when a very drunk sailor, who was a notoriously angry man, came to us, and he told all the people in the room to shut up, and he told a few men if they didn't get out of the room, he'd kill them. I was serving soup and bread, and I went to him and told him he was a great friend to us that day, and we were grateful, *very* grateful. He looked at me. I'll never forget those blue eyes of his; they were moving away from me, then closing in on me; they were dancing all over, then they were so still and penetrating I was more afraid of them than any knife or gun he may have had. His hair was long, for those days, and he would move his right hand through the thick, curly hair and then he'd wipe the hand on his trousers, as if he'd touched something dirty. Mind you, his trousers were fairly dirty themselves. He saw me following that hand, looking at his trousers, and he bellowed, 'What are you looking at?' There were some swear words in the question. I knew our only hope was to be as quick and decisive and as honest with him as I could possibly be. I said, 'At you.' He shouted back, 'Why are you looking at me?' I answered, 'Because I'm standing here talking with you.' He shouted back, 'Well, who are you?' I gave him my name and asked him who he was. He told me – his first name, at least, Fred. I offered my hand to him, and he offered his, but before he let us shake, he asked me if I was worried that he was dirty. I said no, and besides, I hadn't washed my own hands, and there was all sorts of crud on them, from the kitchen, and would he excuse me, and he said yes, and then we shook.

"Then I took the initiative. I thanked him. I said he had just been a lifesaver. He gave me a strange look. He lowered his eyes, stared at the floor, and talked to me without looking at me. He said he *didn't* want to be called a lifesaver, I must not call him that. He was growling, and I was more frightened then than I had been earlier, when he was shouting, and the whole room was terrified. I decided *not* to explain my use of the word, the phrase. This was no time for a lecture on colloquial English. I asked him if I could give him some soup. He asked me what was in it. I told him lots of good vegetables. He asked me if I would have some. I said I was hungry, and I sure would. So we sat down, and he wouldn't start until I did. He watched me swallow a few tablespoons, and then he was about to start his, when all of a sudden he changed his mind and asked me if he could have *my* soup. I said sure, and he gobbled it up!

"Meanwhile, I had a flash of an intuition, because I saw him staring at his soup! I asked him if I could have that soup. He said yes, that he *wanted* me to have it, as a matter of fact. He was growling again. I took the bowl and slurped it up, hungrily. I *was* hungry. He sat there watching me, as intently as I had ever been watched. The whole room was silent – the strangest silence I think we had ever had in any Catholic Worker soup kitchen. As I was finishing the bowl I began to realize what was going on in his head. I put the bowl down. His eyes moved from me to the bowl. I asked him if there was anything else he wanted. He didn't answer me. I told him I was very happy to meet him, and then I turned to another man, sitting nearby, and asked him how he was doing. Before he could answer, the big man I had just been talking to had come nearer to me, and it must have seemed to some people in the room that he was going to attack me, to hurt me.

"He was growling a bit, making noises like a dog does. I looked at him, and he stared at me. I remember what took place as clearly as if it happened yesterday. I could only think of one thing – what I had learned long ago, reading the Bible, years before I became a Catholic, the King James Version: 'Be

not overcome of evil, but overcome evil with good.' They are
the last words of the twelfth chapter of Paul's letter to the
Romans. That chapter was one of Peter's favorites, and is one
of my favorites. I read it at least once every few days, sometimes over and over again. I spoke those words to myself – 'Be
not overcome of evil, but overcome evil with good' – and I
smiled at that man. He didn't smile back. I picked up a piece of
bread, broke it in half, took part of one half in my mouth, and
offered him the other half – and he took it. He said thank you,
and I said (trying to appear as relaxed and casual as possible),
'Oh, do come here, anytime; we'd love to have you as our
guest.' Then I excused myself. I said I had to go get us some
vegetables for tomorrow's soup. He sat down and finished his
bread. As I left, I could hear the room getting noisier and noisier,
and I'll tell you, I was never happier to hear all that rattle, all that
racket in that dining room of ours. Do you know what? The next
day that man came early in the morning with bags full of celery
and carrots and onions and potatoes. I asked him, please, to
come and have lunch, taste the soup with his vegetables in it, and
he said he would. He became one of our regulars."

She stopped at that point, got up and looked at a pile of books on
a table across the room. She found a copy of the New English Bible.
A friend had given it to her. We talked about the language in that
Bible, the language in the King James Version, with which we had
both grown up. I told her that I had resisted the New English Bible
for a long time, but read it more and more, though I still primarily
call upon the King James Version. She gave me a bit of a lecture on
the Catholic church and the Bible and told me she still had what some
of her Catholic friends call a Protestant streak: her intense love of
the Bible, her constant reading of it, her willingness to let it be so
much a source of comfort. Those friends had told her that "true
Catholics get their solace out of church, not reading the Bible."

She then talked about Saint Paul – about that beautiful twelfth
chapter of his Epistle to the Romans. She remembered the many
times she and others she knew had read that chapter. It offers a

powerful sanction to the idea of community, which the Catholic Worker Movement has emphasized as central to its moral and social philosophy. She picked up the New English Bible and read aloud the entire twelfth chapter, beginning with its title, "Christian Behavior." She told me, afterward, that she used to resent some of those titles, but this one had won her over. "It is exactly what Paul was trying to describe, to exhort his correspondents to achieve." She reminded me that the thirteenth verse of the twelfth chapter urges this. "Contribute to the needs of God's people, and practice hospitality." She read aloud a few more verses, those that follow the thirteenth one. "Call down blessings on your persecutors – blessings, not curses. / With the joyful be joyful, and mourn with the mourners. / Care as much about each other as about yourselves. Do not be haughty, but go about with humble talk. Do not keep thinking how wise you are."

That last line prompted her to remember the old days, the secular days, the Greenwich Village days of her life. She had met so many "wise" people but had noticed a good deal of self-importance in many of those wise ones, and in herself.

"When you get older you remember with regret as well as nostalgia. Many young people picture themselves to be immortal, so they are well along the road of arrogance. Young *bright* people are even further along – all those smart thoughts to show to others. Young, bright, *idealistic* people are tempted in a special way by arrogance. The ambition they have to change the world can turn into a bullying of others and a terrible habit of patronizing everyone but themselves. I wasn't all that bright, but I could write fairly good articles, and I was full of idealism, and I was a young, politically-conscious person – we thought ourselves to be liberated – and the result was a fairly swollen head, I'm afraid. As I keep reading Paul's Letter to the Romans, that twelfth chapter, I can't help remembering those years of the early 1920s with some shame.

"But there is no point dwelling on the past excessively. My mother used to warn us against that; she'd say, 'Doting on what's gone is wasting precious time.' It's stealing time, really, from the present and from the future. If you believe in the mission of Jesus Christ, then you're bound to try to let go of your past, in the sense that you are entitled to His forgiveness. To keep regretting what was is to deny God's grace. I know someone who tells me all the time that she's not worthy of becoming a Catholic, that Christianity is beyond her because of all the terrible things she has said and done in her life, especially her youth. I try to talk with her about such pride, try to show her the many mischievous forms it takes, but she is adamant. In a terrible way, I think she is still thinking how wise she is, as Saint Paul put it, meaning, in her case, holding on to the importance of her analysis of her earlier life. We are all of us too smart for our own good."

She stopped, frowned, and then smiled. She wanted to point out another part of that wonderful twelfth chapter of Romans. She sat there, holding the Bible, reading it; then she read aloud the passages she considered to be a guide for living in a house of hospitality:

In virtue of the gift that God in His grace has given me I say to everyone among you: do not be conceited or think too highly of yourself; but think your way to a sober estimate based on the measure of faith that God has dealt to each of you. For just as in a single human body there are many limbs and organs, all with different functions, so all of us, united with Christ, form one body, serving individually as limbs and organs to one another.

The gifts we possess differ as they are allotted to us by God's grace, and must be exercised accordingly: the gift of inspired utterances, for example, in proportion to a man's faith; or the gift of administration, in administration. A teacher should employ his gift of teaching, and one who has the gift of stirring speech should use it to stir his hearers. If you give to charity, give with all your heart; if you are a leader, exert yourself to lead; if you are helping others in distress, do it cheerfully.

Love in all sincerity, loathing evil and clinging to the good. Let love for our brotherhood breed warmth of mutual affection. Give pride of place to one another in esteem.

These passages, she pointed out, carried "about all there is to say" with respect to the "philosophy" that guides the hospitality houses. I had been asking her to spell out this philosophy, and though she had mentioned Teresa of Avila and Francis of Assisi and the Bible, I hadn't quite stopped asking the question, perhaps because I was trying to connect the kind of living I had observed in those houses with a more contemporary rationale. However, the strength of feeling she conveyed in reading that twelfth chapter of Romans, the obvious dedication of thought she had given to those words of Saint Paul, persuaded me at last that this "modern" woman was guided by a thoroughly biblical sensibility.

Dorothy Day had told me many times that at "low" moments she found herself going to the Bible with a need, a desperation which frightened her. What did she mean? Why was she frightened by her affection for and reliance on the Old and New Testaments? She explained:

"I was frightened in general – the life I left for the new life I was living. I had been a solitary person in certain ways, and now I was a member of a community. I yearned for the change, but I was also scared by the change. I had never known the kind of life I began living once we were running a hospitality house in New York. There were times when I wanted to take my daughter and run, but I didn't want to run, not really. That's what I mean by frightened. I was anxious, I was scared, but I was going to stay there and do the work I needed to do.

"Whenever I became *too* jittery I read the Bible. First the Bible would come to my mind, then I would go get it, then I'd read it. You will probably call me superstitious or childish, but sometimes I would just close my eyes and let my hand stumble to a certain page, and then read what I first saw when my eyes opened. I thought it was God, showing me what I needed to see that day. I knew better, but I loved just accidentally opening the book to this page or that page and connecting what I had read to what was happening in my life. Once, by accident, I found that chapter from Romans open on my table two days in a row. First I thought I had left the book open, but I hadn't. Then I was going to ask all the people I could who had been reading my Bible, but I calmed down, and realized that I ought to go read Saint Paul's second letter to the Corinthians, when he talks about the difference between the letter and the spirit. I was behaving like a detective, maybe because I was afraid to believe that God might have wanted to send a message to me. But who dares take for granted God is that near?

"The Bible helps me get through the painful times of this life, reminds me of what I am doing here. There are days when I'm not feeling too well, and I dream of having a small Greenwich Village apartment, one of those top-floor ones, with the sun shining in, and a good view of the sky, with lots of plants and books and a cat, maybe, and comfortable chairs and my own kitchen, where I could cook up a storm sometimes, just for myself! I picture myself sipping coffee and reading and, yes, smoking cigarettes. Dear God, I was a terrible smoker. It's amazing that my lungs are still here. I stopped, eventually, just before becoming a burnt-out case. But I don't judge myself wicked for such thoughts. I used to – I would call myself selfish and spoiled. Think of the people, all the people all over the world, who have never enjoyed the comforts I have had and who don't get distracted by remembering them."

She was too shrewd to let herself get away with such a comparison. She pointed out – to herself as much as to me – that those who have lived unrelievedly desperate lives are nevertheless capable of constructing rather elaborate fantasies of an alternative life for themselves. We can all picture a better place to be. She then continued to discuss the satisfactions and the irritations of the kind of living she pursued most of her adult life. She reminded me that she did have escapes – that she traveled a lot, almost always by bus, to lecture or attend lectures, to take part in demonstrations or protests. She reminded me that there was a network of hospitality houses, each with its own "tone" or climate, each stressing a particular aspect of Catholic Worker thought. She reminded me, for instance, that there are urban hospitality houses and rural ones; that there are soup kitchens and farms; that there are houses which work mostly with white people, and others with black or Spanish-speaking people. (The Houston *Catholic Worker* is published in both Spanish and English.[5]) She reminded me, too, that, one winter, she had gone on "retreat" to Staten Island – to one of two cottages owned by Catholic Workers, a refuge near the water.

The question of property, the matter of privacy – these two issues had troubled her during all her Catholic Worker years. They are issues for anyone who has lived in a hospitality house. She had no trouble, mostly, "closing the door" on others, though she would remind herself of the millions of people who can't take even a room or a door for granted. Nevertheless, she was quick to stand up for her personal requirements, which to her were compatible with the idea of a community.

"A community is not a place where 'desert fathers' are testing themselves – more and more, harder and harder, each on his own. A community is what Saint Paul told us – our differences granted respect by one another, but those differences not allowed to turn us into loners. You must know when to find your own, quiet moment of solitude. But you must know when to open the door to go be with others, and you must know *how* to open the door. There's no point in opening the door with bitterness and resentment in your heart. I have noticed that those alcoholics, those bums and tramps and ne'er-do-wells have a way of reading our faces, getting quickly to the truth of our souls. They do that, I fear, better than we do with one another. We try to protect one another, we 'cover' for one another – oh, maybe we don't want to see in each other what we don't want to see in the privacy of our own rooms, staring into the mirror: our sins at work in our lives.

"I remember one day realizing that the best, the very best, I could do for everyone in the community, including our guests at lunch, was to stay away, not to fight staying away, which I might have done successfully. There are times when one's generosity is a mask for one's pride: what will 'they' do without me, without my energy put at their disposal? Peter, dear Peter never seemed to have such questions eating away at him. He had less ego than just about anyone I've ever met. He would orate; he would go and try to capture an audience for his words, so, at first, you'd want to think of him as an egotist who has found a master in Jesus. But after you would come to know him and watch him at work, you would realize that he wasn't using language, written or spoken, for himself. The words came out of him the way love comes from us, if we're full of love, a kind of outpouring of trust and affection. He was giving, *giving* those words, and he didn't want a return on them in the form of an I O U from his listeners and readers: you're great, Peter."

She apologized for her murkiness and rather unscientific psychology. She then mentioned flaws in Peter's character, a certain vagueness and helter-skelter behavior which put burdens on others. As for herself, she had struggled hard for years, she said, to achieve a certain selflessness, until she had come to realize that the very struggle was a contradiction. All she could do, finally, was try to be true to her decent, honorable side, knowing there was another side. To battle one side with the energy and resourcefulness of the other side was to wage, as she put it, "the wrong war for the wrong reasons." She clarified her conclusion in this manner:

"To fight vanity is to yield to it, an aphorism I used to hear from Forster, who got tired of my mention of vanity and tired of my quotations from Saint Augustine. He once told me that if I would just relax and try to be myself, I would be less at the mercy of the vanity that was worrying me. That was a pretty complicated psychology at work, and he wasn't supposed to be interested in psychology, and he was supposed to be taciturn

and silently introspective. I try to remember his advice, and
sometimes I even think it has helped me a lot."

She was a writer, hence her worry about her use of those words
faith and *love* and *charity*; she knew how banal and hollow anyone's language can be as it tries to do justice to moral and spiritual
yearning. No wonder she summoned the Bible as an ally so often.
Several times as she tried to explain her everyday life at St. Joseph's
House in the early 1970s, she quoted to me from the second
chapter of Paul's Epistle to the Philippians; I had heard her read
from that section of Philippians years earlier, in the late 1950s.
As she read the words one could feel the urgency in her voice, as
if she were talking to herself, reminding herself, teaching herself
an all-important lesson, an imperative that would hold her life
together.

> If then our common life in Christ yields anything to stir the
> heart, any loving consolation, any sharing of the Spirit, any
> warmth of affection or compassion, fill up my cup of happiness
> by thinking and feeling alike, with the same love for one
> another, the same turn of mind, and a common care for unity.
> There must be no room for rivalry and personal vanity among
> you, but you must humbly reckon others better than your-
> selves. Look to each other's interest and not merely to your
> own.
>   Let your bearing towards one another arise out of your life in
> Christ Jesus. For the divine nature was His from the first; yet
> He did not think to snatch at equality with God, but made
> Himself nothing, assuming the nature of a slave.

She then skipped forward to these lines: "'So you too, my friends,
must be obedient, as always; even more, now that I am away, than
when I was with you. You must work out your own salvation in
fear and trembling; for it is God who works in you, inspiring both
the will and the deed, for his own chosen purpose.

She took that message to heart, kept trying to follow it. She kept markers in her Bible, and often singled out that passage from Philippians. She had the "curse of impatience," she was quite convinced. She believed it ironic that as she grew older those who regarded her from the distance of their youth remarked constantly on her forbearance, her stoic endurance, her seeming ability to tolerate so much that struck them as extremely irritating. In her mind, in her memories, she was still the unruly one, trying to settle down and feel easy and open with others. She also saw herself as possessive, not as eager to share with others as she wished she might be. She had many incidents in her past to "live down," as she once put it, and even in her last years she would talk about the books she "owned," hated to lend, and kept hidden, lest they be borrowed by others without permission. The struggle to be obedient and the struggle against rivalry which Saint Paul mentions, were hers, she well knew; the struggle to be part of a common life was also hers.

That phrase "common life," intrigued her. She loved the two senses of common, as in ordinary and as in shared. She had once sought celebrity and was aware that even as she had tried to forsake the self-assertiveness of the writer, the secular intellectual, in favor of an intensely religious life, spent among the poor, she had gradually become well known for her work, for the way she lived her life: a quiet celebrity, much read, much visited, much celebrated by young people as well as by those of her own generation.

She was not afraid to reflect on that outcome:

"I am still a journalist, for the good, I hope, but also because the 'old Adam' is in me.[6] I guess that phrase of George Eliot's should have its woman's equivalent, the 'old Eve.' I still get excited when we have a fight to wage and the world pays attention. I'm still ready to stay up late and try to figure out the best way to say something so that more and more people will pay attention. When important people – writers, political folks – come here and want to learn what we're doing, one side of me is impressed. I can feel my blood warming. I'm ready to meet them halfway, more than halfway. Peter's advice is in my head, his way of thinking: teach them, or as he put it, 'indoctrinate' them, and they will do the same with others, and on and on and on. He didn't use the word *indoctrinate* the way we do, now. He used it in the sense of teaching so that the person really remembers, feels, takes to heart. If the rich and powerful and influential get converted, well, that is wonderful, he would say: God's grace has befallen them. If we can help things along, wonderful, he would say, again.

"I wasn't so sure then, and I'm not so sure now. Our pride, our vanity, responds to the interest of important people. People tell me we're becoming important and a force in the church; they tell me the pope admires us; they tell me I'm going to be a saint one of these days, and I don't know whether to laugh or to cry. I hear such talk and I feel sad, mostly. I go to my room and read. I'll take the Bible and read it or one of my novels; or I'll try to sit and talk with someone in our community who needs a listener. If I were really free of the worst sin of them all, pride, I would not be upset by such talk. I'd forget it very quickly and get on with my work. I'm here to help out with all my strength, until I die – help out in this house of hospitality, our community here. I'm *not* here to spend my time being better and better known by people who like to applaud certain people and debunk others. 'Your movement is getting more and more recognition,' an old friend once told me, and I answered her right away. 'Look, it's not *my* movement, and I'm wondering *who* is recognizing us. God? The numerous agents the devil has? And recognized for what?' She thought I was being too defensive, but I have always thought that a certain kind of success could be a sign of our ruin. We are meant to be with the poor – those of us who have chosen to live here – and the distractions of the mighty should be a warning to us: that we not be blinded by their glitter."

When she had finished with that small oration she put on her glasses, which had been placed on a table to her right. Only when she reached for them did I notice that she had not been wearing them for a while. With them firmly in place, she seemed sharply observant – not "blind," certainly – and not the least bit likely to be diverted by glitter.

Still, I wondered about the darker side of a life spent in the various houses of hospitality. In her writing and in conversations she acknowledged her irritable and selfish moments, as well as the preoccupations which kept her from her own child. What does it mean to bring up a child in a hospitality house? As a child psychiatrist trained to uphold the virtues of a traditional family and a traditional environment, I become concerned at the thought of a little girl watching incoherent and alcoholic and depressed and agitated people day in and day out. On the other hand, there is the possibility of a warm larger family in the hospitality houses. There is also the fact that difficult childhoods and mental casualties are often found among the comfortable and psychologically oriented families of our conventional American suburbs.

Sometimes, as I've talked with children who live in those suburbs,[7] I think of Dorothy Day's descriptions of Tamar's childhood in *The Long Loneliness*, and conclude that "growing up in community," as she calls it in that book, probably did not put her psychologically at risk. All those friends, those priests and brothers and nuns, those idealistic youths, they loved Dorothy and Tamar and gave them their continuing energy. At a novitiate run by the Marist Fathers, one Father McKenna took a particular interest in them. "He loved Tamar and took her around with him to the barns, to watch the brothers milk the cows and feed the chickens, and she was devoted to him. She found a nest of field mice when they were cutting hay and brought them in to make homes for them in muffin tins. She helped Brother Philip water the garden with a little sprinkler." There are many other such fetching images, and they are instructive for some of us with narrow views of what is necessary or desirable for children. A few more Brother Philips for us and our children and who knows how their lives – or our moral lives – might turn out.

7

Her Spiritual Kin

No one who has spent any time reading Dorothy Day or speaking with her or looking at her library and the books she kept close to her would have any great difficulty figuring out which writers meant the most to her in the course of her extraordinary life. She lived ardently with the Bible, with the Hebrew prophets and their sense of moral outrage in the face of injustice, and, of course, with Jesus, whose earthly ministry she never stopped contemplating and holding up as an example for her own life. She often turned to particular saints, to Teresa of Avila and Thérèse of Lisieux, John of the Cross, Saint Francis of Assisi, and Catherine of Siena for inspiration in the face of many hurdles.[1]

Novelists also figured predominantly in her life, especially, as already noted, the nineteenth-century ones, Dickens, Dostoievski, and Tolstoy. She loved Dickens's effort to bring the poor to the attention of his readers,[2] Dostoievski's religious fervor and philosophical subtlety,[3] Tolstoy's largeness of mind and heart.[4] She also loved Chekhov, his wry yet tender stance with regard to a suffering and perplexed humanity.[5]

She was an almost feverish reader, who once called herself hungry for books. She saw her literary side as a mixed blessing.

"When Tamar was young, I was always being tempted by books during our spare time together, and we didn't have all that much spare time. A friend of mine once told me she had to close her eyes when she walked past a bar; I told her I knew how she felt. I have to close my eyes when I walk by a bookstore and even a library. I could have 'binges' of reading, 'lost weekends' of reading, if I didn't watch out."

Still, by her "spiritual kin" I don't mean a recitation of her reading habits. I have in mind those men and women who have struggled in this century to be loyal to a blend of moral and political virtue, an espousal of ideals that becomes an everyday commitment of energy and intelligence. Writers, though, even those whom Dorothy Day much admired, haven't usually spent their lives living in places like hospitality houses. Even her friend Jacques Maritain,[6] who helped her connect a philosophical and theological Catholicism to the existential kind she and Peter Maurin had made, was not able to live his life as she did, with one foot in the world of writing and ideas and the other in the world of urban soup kitchens, rural communities, and picket lines. Her monthly column, "On Pilgrimage," was written for a newspaper aimed not at intellectuals but ordinary working people.

I once asked Dorothy Day about the company she hoped to keep in the next world and about spiritual kinship she felt in this life. Her reply was particularly revealing.

"I know that we're all educated to think highly of presidents and generals, actors and actresses, rich men and geniuses, all sorts of geniuses. We're educated to look up to people who have made a lot of money or who have become successful in some way – maybe written important novels or poems or composed music that people like a lot or been artists who have done something special. I'm like everyone else: I admire people who have become outstanding. I have read a novel, and thought to myself, I'd like to meet that writer, or I wish I could write the way that writer has written. I have felt the envy or frustration; pure admiration doesn't last long. But if it's the company I seek that you're asking about, I'll answer the question like this. I'll say that I'm no factory worker or farmer, but I think of factory workers and farmers when I write and when I read and when I'm in church. Remember, we are called Catholic *Workers*. We're not called Catholic Intellectuals or Catholic Literary People or Catholic Social Activists or Catholic Revolutionaries or a Catholic Political Action Group. Peter was a 'laboring man'; he was as plain and hard working as you could want; he had used his hands, his strength to make a living; he had planted crops and harvested them. He helped pull me away from people who *talk* about working people so that I could spend my life with people who *are* working people. I don't think of myself as a leader of those people or as their teacher or as some important authority they should have in their lives. I think of myself as – one of them.

"I remember once, I was sitting and eating lunch, and several of the men we had served came up to me and asked me if they could sit and talk. Certainly. They asked me why we had crosses in the room, and religious stuff. I explained that we prayed a lot to God, thanked Him for His kindness to us. They weren't convinced there is a God, and they said that *if* there is one, then He hasn't done a very good job. I asked them what they meant. They said that He has let the poor get poorer and the rich get richer. I didn't know what to say about that. Then one of the men said he didn't care if that's what has happened. He said, 'Look, here we are, and we're together here, and we'll be together in heaven, too, if there is a heaven.' Then he asked me if I believed 'that.' I wasn't sure what he was meaning, so I asked him what question he wanted me to answer. I was hoping he would phrase the question so that I could say something sensible. He asked me whether I thought that God would keep us together, all of us sitting there, then, and all the people who came to eat our food – would He send us to one part of His Kingdom, and send other people to some other part?

"I didn't know the answer to his question for a few seconds. I just sat there, silent, wondering what to say. Then another man answered for me; he said that God had already separated us here, and we would be sticking together up there as well, because we belong together. I have never forgotten that moment. I believe that as I die, I'll be remembering that man's words. I believe God may have helped him speak to us that day. Peter once told me that he expected us all to be together in the next life; he was sure of it. I can't be as sure as he was. But I hope and pray we all stay in this big Catholic Worker family. We are relatives – kinfolk, some would say: those who receive, give; and those who give, receive. But I am not telling you anything new."

Dorothy Day was determined to make herself a constant companion to people for whom, earlier in her life, she had felt a more remote concern or compassion. Now "they" had become quite something else to her.

"When I was young I would wake up and wonder about the new people I'd see or what new and interesting thing I might end up doing. I would be full of new plans, and I would be interested in the newest ideas. I'd want to read everything 'new and interesting': those words always went together. Then we got our Catholic Worker family going, and all of us have the same kind of lives. We aren't looking for new twists on this life. We're not hoping to meet so-and-so and then a new so-and-so. We've already met everyone who counts – the Lord and those who followed Him, His disciples, and some of the saints of the church, who help remind us what He was really like. And we've met one another here in St. Joseph's House or in other hospitality houses, and we know that together we're all that any of us could ever hope to find: a big bunch of 'fools for Christ.' We're foolish kin, you might call us."

In her intimate life with the Bible, certain figures stand out: Saint Paul and his evocation of the absurdity of Christian thinking, its way of overturning conventional assumptions, and such Hebrew prophets as Jeremiah and Isaiah and Amos.[7] It is too easy, perhaps, for those in the secular world who admire her to overlook this intense biblical side of her intellectual life. We are intrigued by her political and social views but miss the extent of her interest in, say, Thérèse of Lisieux or John of the Cross.[8] She knew what effect her preoccupations could have.

"I find some of the church's saints taking up more of my time than is good for me. My friends tell me I want to go back to earlier ages of the church, and they're right. I would love to have been here when Saint Francis was with us. I don't mean that I would love to meet him the way that word is used these days. I guess I mean that he's still with us, and I'm sure he could teach us even more if we were able to be nearby and be witnesses to what he did and how he did what he did. Sometimes it's not the deed, but the manner of the deed.

"The other day I was getting ready to serve some of our guests, and I didn't feel very good-hearted, I'm sorry to say. I had a bit of a stomachache, and I was worried about something, too. When I woke up that morning I had thought to myself, This is one of those days when you would do everyone a favor, including yourself, if you would stay in bed. But I wasn't going to be that generous. I got up and set to work doing my chores. When the time came to serve the people, I wasn't really noticing them, or paying any attention to what might be happening in that room. I was lost in my own selfish world, I'm afraid to say. Suddenly, I heard a man — one of our regulars — talking to me. He was brusque, but he obviously wanted to be of help to me. He said, 'Can I do something for you?' I was surprised, and I'm afraid the devil had taken over me, because I shot back at him, 'No! Why do you ask?' I was annoyed, and he knew it. He may have been drinking, but I was the one who was 'out of it.' I was all wrapped up in my own world; I was thinking of some poems I had read the night before, and I was ignoring the people who had come to us for some food.

"I could feel my stomach hurting as I stood there, ready to find an excuse to move away from that man, but he wouldn't let me go. He told me he knew me – he'd been to us many times – and he was worried about me. That's when I really noticed my stomach was hurting, and that's when I thought of Thérèse of Lisieux and all the pain she had to endure and how bravely she did so. I couldn't get her out of my mind for the rest of the day. It was as if she were standing there, beside me, telling me to cheer up and smile and pray to God and my prayers would be answered. I asked the man to sit down, and I got him some coffee and some for myself, and we started to talk. It was a wonderful talk. He really had been noticing my moods. He had noticed all of us – our ups and downs. I thought to myself, *He* is the one who is trying to be of help to others, and *we* are the ones who need that help.

"People come and tell us that we're doing a good job, but they don't stop and think about who is enabling us to do that job. I don't mean by just being there; I mean by reaching out to us, the way that man reached out to me. He sat there telling me how great it feels when one of our community offers a bowl of soup to him, looking right at him, smiling, and saying a friendly word or two, and how down in the dumps he feels when the soup or the coffee is dished out and we're off in some other world while we're doing the dishing out. I remember Peter saying that any one of those people who come to see us might be Jesus Himself, or one of His disciples, or one of His saints, but at that moment I was truly convinced that the Lord had made that old man a deputy of His, had dispatched him to put us in our place."

In other conversations she described similar times in which she had not done as much for others as she might have wished, only to be prompted by some incident to stop and think of a particular passage in the Bible, a particular saint's life. Sometimes she would stop, close her eyes, and carry on a conversation with that saint. She was not talking about visions or hallucinations. She was talking about her sense that there is the company of saints for all of us to keep if we want. She thought that a believer feels a bond with others who have struggled with life's mysteries. The saints, for her, were men and women who had waged such a struggle, and their losses, their pain and uncertainty, as well as their victories, their moments of moral satisfaction or religious ecstasy, are an inheritance from which all of us are eligible to draw.

"I think I talk in my sleep to God and to the saints," she once said; and then she added:

"I *know* I talk to them when I'm awake all the time. When people try to be nice to me and tell me that they've noticed I am doing a bit of talking to myself, I always deny it. I tell them that I'm *not* talking to myself, I'm talking to someone else: to our dear Lord, to His Son, to those who gave their lives for them, the saints of the church. Some people laugh, but I'm being as serious as I know how to be. There are days when I've not talked much to anyone who is alive, but I've talked plenty to people who once were alive and now have departed for the sight of God. I don't dare say I've heard *them* talking. What I hear is my voice remembering *their* words. I hope what I'm saying makes me not quite 'a case,' not a fanatic, only some aging lady who is religiously obsessed."

While communicating in this way with religious figures of the past, Dorothy Day also sought support from contemporary writers or political activists who shared her ideals. I heard her talk about Orwell, about Ignazio Silone, about Danilo Dolci, about Simone Weil and Edith Stein, and about Dietrich Bonhoeffer.[9] She had great admiration for Orwell on several counts. She loved his accounts of his "down-and-out" life in London and Paris; his report on the condition of mine workers in Wigan during the 1930s; his description of the Spanish civil war. His compassion for the poor, and his ideological struggles with various shades along the left's spectrum elicited her strong interest and prompted long conversations with interested visitors.

She was not afraid or ashamed, however, to be tough on Orwell, to take issue with his writing when she considered it off the mark.

She found some of the passages in *Down and Out in London and Paris* offensively cynical – [10] the ambitious writer learning from the poor, enjoying their vitality, but failing to register the inner melancholy of their lives.

"I don't mean that he didn't describe poverty with great care or that he didn't have great consideration and affection for some of the tramps he met. I'm talking about his own relationship to those tramps: he's quite objective about them, and he's a wonderful storyteller who captures all those revealing moments in great detail. He brings you very close *to* them; but he doesn't help you get *inside* them the way I'd like, the way a novelist who has never been with such people might. I mean, inside their hearts, not their minds! [I had asked for an elaboration.] It's true, he reveals their sardonic humor or their bitterness or their shrewdness, but these are people who have known a lot of pain and who probably haven't (can't, won't) share it with Orwell or anybody else, including themselves. We have our tramps here, and they drink, I often think, because they want to cry and cry and cry, and they don't know how, and so instead of letting tears flow out, they take whiskey in. I'm not saying I have the slightest idea how I would ever do what I wish Orwell could have done, but I know there's another side to those tramps that he didn't quite get."

Though she knew that she was not able to manage his uncanny mix of austerity and energy as a documentary writer, her admiration for Orwell was, I sometimes thought, more qualified than she indicated. When she wanted more "heart" from him and then apologized for her own sentimentality, I would wonder whether she felt a great distance to have existed between Orwell the observer-writer and the people he got to know, and I wondered, too, whether she felt he ought to have put in more time with those people. I was sensitive on that score, having done my own version of "social observation," so one day I asked her about this side of Orwell.

"I have always felt that as an essayist he has no equal. I suppose I wish he were more interested in religion and more interested in the spiritual lives of poor people. When a writer is as great as Orwell was, you want more from him. He's not one of my close spiritual friends, I'd have to say, but when I read *Homage to Catalonia* I remembered myself wandering in the [ideological] wilderness, feeling lost and very confused: someone who lost all the moorings she had been taking for granted and was adrift. When I read *The God That Failed* I thought of *Homage to Catalonia*, though Orwell never did set up communism as a religious faith for himself, the way Koestler and Richard Wright and Silone describe themselves doing. Orwell's aloofness saved him from the very start, but he paid a price, in my book."

In Orwell, Dorothy Day found a friend to an important part of her earlier self, her pre-Catholic self. Put differently, the secular idealism which she had brought to Catholicism was excited by Orwell. Her political nature, her muckraking journalist sensibility, also found him constantly of interest, constantly rewarding to read. He brought back memories to her of the effort she made to align herself all the way with socialism. Yet, like him, she had never quite succeeded in doing so. Both of them had their own way of being stubbornly individualistic and also patriotic. She was as deeply American in certain respects as he was English, and nationalism pulled them from the internationalist spirit of 1920s or 1930s socialism and communism.

Orwell's nationalism, of course, flowered during the Second World War, while she held true to her Christian pacifism. She found in Catholicism her own internationalist "cause"; Orwell died leery of all causes, especially statist ones. He seemed most comfortable with so-called working-class families, whereas she was most comfortable, I suspect, with more humble people who had only religious faith to lean on. They shared a moral disgust at the injustices they couldn't stop noticing, a desire to write about what they saw, and a strong meliorist wish to right as many wrongs as possible, without thereby creating a new series of injustices.

She was much closer to Ignazio Silone, to his personal pilgrimage and to his way of seeing things. As she never tired telling some of us, he was born extremely poor; his father was a peasant, his mother was a weaver – his name, Tranquilli Secondo. (He would become Ignazio Silone, just as Eric Blair became George Orwell.) He was a Catholic. When he was fifteen years old, a terrible earthquake struck the village of Pescina where his family lived. On a January morning some fifty thousand people were killed in a matter of seconds. The Catholic clergy left the scene, part of the privileged class which could escape, while the poor buried their dead, suffered terribly, and prayed to God in their own fashion. Silone survived the disaster and bore witness to an example of religious hypocrisy – cowardice and selfishness hidden by the Roman collar.

Shortly thereafter Silone would leave his native region, begin a trek through the corridors of revolutionary Marxism: enchantment, activism, disenchantment, and finally, a prolonged moral reflection which was shared with the world through writing. Like Dorothy Day he was jailed; he picketed and joined strikes; he engaged in long, tempestuous arguments; he met and was inspired by political and literary people and came to see their warts or sins. Always his heart went out to the *cafoni*, the wretchedly poor, landless people who were Italy's *lumpenproletariat*. Gradually he began to see the devilish intrigue, the betrayals, the lies, the gossip, the malicious maneuvering, and the murders all carried out in the name of the revolution, the people, the cause.

In the late 1920s, well before Stalin's purges, he pulled away from international communism. He went back to his Catholic past, to *its* past. He was enthralled by the story of Pietro da Morrone, the Benedictine monk who became Pope Celestino V for a few months in the year 1294. An exceptionally religious man, he was utterly unable to become an able administrator, never mind a wheeler-dealer politician and head of state. After five months of rule he resigned, the only pope ever to do so, obviously too Christ-like for the institution of which he had been made leader. Silone and Dorothy Day appreciated that irony enormously – the incompatibility between a Christian saint and the church that claims to

146

have been founded by Jesus Christ himself. Dorothy Day loved to meditate on that pope and on Silone's latter-day response to him. She thought of that brief papacy as a flash of heavenly light upon the church, upon mankind's religious history: how ill at ease, how out of place true virtue is in the world. The community which had once consisted of Jesus and His disciples and those drawn to them had turned into an enormous bureaucracy, with deals and favors and patronage and greed and crookedness and double-crossing and bribery, to the point that a devout and decent man was unable to comprehend it all or survive in the midst of such a state of affairs.

Pietro Spina, the central figure in *Bread and Wine*,[11] a revolutionary who has had to go underground in fascist Italy and does so in the disguise of a priest, was connected in Silone's mind to this thirteenth-century monk. Dorothy Day was entranced by the book and enjoyed the irony of a leftist political leader on the run from a brutal right-wing regime, masquerading as a priest and proving himself to be a wonderfully sensitive and thoughtful person whose words and deeds fit right into the Christian tradition. Just as in Dorothy Day's account of her own journey, *From Union Square to Rome*, the direction of *Bread and Wine* is from politics to the love people can offer each other as members of a community.

Companionship in its literal meaning is "the sharing of bread," and several times, as she contemplated a lunch scene at St. Joseph's House – people offering and receiving bread (and soup and coffee) – she mentioned *Bread and Wine*, speaking of its powerful significance to her and the "comradeship" she felt with Silone.[12] His moral, political, and religious search is worked into the texture of the novel, and she responded to it with her own moments of self-examination. She spotted his loneliness, sensitized by her own. When Cristina Colamartini, the ascetic and religiously meditative woman sets out across the countryside in search of the departed Spina, who has fled the Fascists, and is promptly beset by wolves, a reader such as Dorothy Day knows full well the author's intent: a statement about the jungle called the civilized world. Cristina's spirituality, her interest in a convent life, was Dorothy Day's; but Bianchina, another woman whom the revolutionary become priest counsels, is sensually alive, even lusty, and Dorothy Day was such a woman, also.

For Dorothy Day the great struggle was to bridge those two sides of herself, to pull together the instinctual and the spiritual, to avoid casual greed and carelessness, yet avoid an intellectual or religious life totally removed from everyday life. Several times over the years I sat and heard Dorothy Day read Spina's words to Cristina with emotion that made her voice tremble.

> If ever a peasant succeeds in overcoming his animal instincts, he becomes a Franciscan friar; if a girl ever succeeds in freeing herself from bondage to her own body, she becomes a nun: Do you not think that is the source of many evils? Do you not think that this divorce between a spirituality which retires into contemplation and a mass of people dominated by animal instincts is the source of all our ills?

In another scene she much loved, the Marxist Spina – become Father Don Paolo – is described while going on his priestly rounds. He is tired of public rallies, of political sermons. He wants a direct intimacy with another person. "Two men must be alone together, talk softly and with many pauses." He sees a youth who is "barefooted, badly dressed, tall and thin." He lives in a wretched shack. They go there, and for a moment the priest returns to his old, messianic Marxist self, extolling the Soviet Russian dream – but then something happens: the intervention of grace, of a person being with another person in a manner that makes politics a footnote to the journey toward human understanding. These words of Silone's, too, prompted Dorothy Day's eyes to fill.

> The young man cut some corn bread, sliced two tomatoes and an onion, and offered them to the priest with a piece of bread. There were still traces of earth on his swollen, scarred hands. The knife he cut the bread with looked as if it were used for everything. Don Paolo shut his eyes and tried to swallow the bread.

"There is a land," he said, "a great land, in which the peasants of the country have joined with the workers of the city."

Meanwhile Matalena [an innkeeper] has been going from house to house, searching for her lodger. At last she found him.

"Dinner has been ready for an hour," she said.

"I'm not hungry," Don Paolo said. "Go back to the inn, because my friend and I have a lot to talk about yet."

"But haven't you noticed he's deaf and dumb and only understands signs?" Matalena asked.

The young man was sitting at the threshold of his hovel, beside the priest. Don Paolo looked him in the face, and saw that his eyes were slowly filling with tears. "It doesn't matter. Go back to the inn. I'm not hungry," the priest said to Matalena.

The two men remained seated at the threshold of the hovel, alone; the one with the gift of speech was silent now, too. Every now and then the two looked at each other and smiled. Day had faded into evening, and now night came. Don Paolo coughed once or twice. The deaf-mute got up, fetched the blanket that covered his straw mattress, and carefully put it around his guest's shoulders. Then Don Paolo remembered that this man would have to get up early in the morning and go to work, so he arose, shook hands with him, and bade him goodnight.

Once, after she had read these words, Dorothy Day looked around her room with its simple furniture, its quiet interrupted occasionally by street noise or the voices of her fellow workers. There were days, she confided, when her mind wandered to past years, when she remembered more comfortable and more private lodgings, when she asked herself why in the world she was living the kind of life she lived. Sometimes, when she began to talk about her doubts, her yearnings, she asked that I not let "that machine" record them. Yet, it was often in connection with a literary discussion that she was particularly open and forthright. Never did I find her more helpful than during those moments when she had *Bread and Wine* near her, when she was under its spell. On one occasion when I went to see her, she read me, with great pleasure, this passage from an essay of Silone's, "The Choice of Companions":

> The spiritual condition I have described allows of no boasting
> . . . It resembles a camp of refugees in some no man's land, out
> in the open, existing by chance. What do you expect refugees
> to do from morning to night? They spend the best part of their
> time telling each other their stories. The stories are not
> very entertaining, to be sure, but they tell them anyhow —
> mainly, to understand what has happened.

She was herself an inspired storyteller, and especially so in dialogue with one other person. She also sought silent moments with herself or with a visitor when she would pray, sit quietly, her hand on the Bible, and pause in the midst of talk to take stock, to think of how a conversation connected to her work.

"When I've read a passage from *Bread and Wine*, or *Homage to Catalonia*, I think of so many people who can't even read at all — what they've missed. I wish I could spend the rest of my life with those people, giving them the bread and wine that is *Bread and Wine*. I wish I could sit with them and tell them what I believe, that God has His eyes on them, and I wish I could hear their thoughts and ideas, their suggestions for me.

"There are some days when I feel that we have made a big mistake — always writing what we think, for others to read, always telling the world what we want to see happen. Silone knew that the deaf and dumb young man had something extremely important to teach Spina: the silence of long-suffering humanity that ought to humble us talkers and writers.

"There was a man I knew when I was young. He was hardly deaf or dumb, but he did have that tall, thin, wild look Silone gives to the deaf and dumb man of *Bread and Wine*. I have never written a word about him, and I didn't know him as well as I knew other men; I knew him in a different way: he would approach me at parties and tell me that he thought we were both lost souls, but he was sure I would be 'found,' whereas he was sure he didn't have time to be 'found.' I didn't know what he meant. I thought he might be sick and soon to die. He was rail thin. But he said, no, he wasn't going to die soon. He said he was a procrastinator, and there simply wasn't enough time in this life – even if he lived to a hundred – to overcome his procrastinator problem. I would laugh, but I could see in his eyes that he really meant what he was saying – that he desperately wanted to be found, but that he'd delay forever being found.

"Once I told him that to be found there has to be someone to find you. He laughed. I thought we were falling in love, and that was our kind of love talk. I was enormously drawn to him, some magic in his face, the delicate features, the premature gray of his hair. (He was only twenty-five; we *both* were twenty-five.) I had him on my mind all the time. I dreamed of being with him – living with him, marrying him, having his children. We would be found together. He would take me on long walks; he'd be silent, not out of shyness or because he had nothing to say, but out of respect for the two of us: the lovely silence that made each of us attracted to the other. I suppose I am getting a bit fuzzy here. It was a sort of sexual silence: the way we both kept all those words inside us and stared at each other or took long walks through the city and then found something to stare at.

"I remember what we once found: a barge, slowly moving down the East River. We followed it as if it was life itself. A sea gull approached it – rose and fell and rose and fell, finally landing and eating and flapping its wings and rising again. Then we noticed an elderly couple sitting and gazing at children, and those children, playing well, and then turning mean, and then making up, and then getting giddy, and then becoming tired and slowing down, and even stopping, each child wiping the eyes or yawning or brushing dirt off the arms: alone, suddenly, for a moment, before getting lost, again, in the little crowd or gang they all were. Oh, and a funeral, I remember that, a long,

long one, with two or three open cars, all full of flowers, and endless people walking, and those cars and some horse-drawn wagons: the tears, the sadness, and a girl who came up to us (she must have been ten, I thought at the time) and told us not to worry, because 'the one who died,' she said, 'is going to heaven.'

"My friend smiled at her with such a big, warm smile that she noticed, she responded to it, to him, to his affection for her, his admiration of her faith – I realize all this now! – and she said to him, 'You'll be going there, too.' I wanted to cry. I thought to myself, What a wonderful father he would make. He spoke, finally – broke the magic of our silence, but just a word: 'I hope so.' He had that big smile on his face, as if he was inviting the dear Lord to come and take him, anytime He wanted; as if he saw an angel of the Lord in that girl, a message from the Almighty that we should have faith and trust in Him.

"We got closer. I was falling in love with him. I *was* in love with him. No [I had asked], his silences weren't brooding; no, they weren't like the ones I described of Forster's [in *The Long Loneliness*]. They were silences I never knew *how* to describe, actually – until I read *Bread and Wine*, that passage [she had just read it aloud, again] between Spina and the deaf-mute young man. I started crying, and I had trouble stopping, when I first came to that passage. I knew Silone was making one of his most important statements ever. All I could do, though, was re-member my friend. He was dead by then; he had been dead for years. He was killed in a train accident. He was not thirty when he died. I heard much later. I had become a Catholic; I prayed for him. Sometimes I would think of him and I would think of Jesus and the saints, the way you do when you read *Bread and Wine*, read Dickens and Dostoievski: *Little Dorrit* or Alyosha in *The Brothers Karamazov*."

When she stopped there was a mixture of joy and sadness on her face. The silence she had been talking about descended on the room, a kind of homage, maybe, to a man, a memory. She took a handkerchief into her hand, but had no cause to use it. She sat there, still and quiet, looking at the line of buildings outside her window, and above them, the sky, on that day partly shielded from view by clouds. With the handkerchief in her right hand she touched her Bible. Then she looked at it. After a few minutes, which seemed to me like a few hours, she started talking again – about spiritual companionship and community, her old standbys, though now with a literary twist.

"Once in a while I'll get a letter from someone who has read something I have written, and I know that it's not a stranger who is writing, but someone I know very well. No [I had asked], I don't really know the person, not in the usual sense of 'know.' But I *do* know the person – so well that I'm a little frightened. When I first 'met' Silone, through his stories, I thought to myself, We're walking down the same road, and we're of the same generation, and that means life is less lonely than I sometimes think. There are days when I get tired, I mean, spiritually weak. It's not that my body is tired – it is, of course, a lot of the time – but that I have very little patience. I have lost whatever 'charity' I have. I have to keep myself on constant alert. I'll wake up, and I'll know the symptoms. I find cynicism taking over my thoughts. I feel like a shrewd skeptic who doesn't much trust people, and is ready to call everyone's bluff. I'll hear people talking, and I want to say, 'Oh yeah, tell us what you *really* have on your mind.'

"I'm shocked by my own arrogance on those mornings. I'll try to say a prayer, immediately: ask God to forgive me, please. If we could only do that more often, ask for His forgiveness. On a *really* bad day I can't seem to do that. I'll forget. I'll be so grouchy – and so grouchy that I'm grouchy – that I live with my grouchiness; I mean, inflict it on everyone else, and only when I'll notice, at last, the hurt in their eyes, do I come to my senses. I go to a room and sit in a corner, like someone who has been sent there by the teacher, and pray for the good Lord to pity me, and give me a reprieve."

153

The theme of forgiveness kept coming up in our talks, as it does in much of the writing she loved. Sometimes she would press me a bit hard on the subject, ask me, for instance, whether I thought forgiveness had a place in psychiatric and psychoanalytic work. I found such a question jarring, hard to answer. I did tell her, on an afternoon in the spring of 1975, about a conversation I had just had weeks earlier with Anna Freud on that very subject.[13] Miss Freud had mentioned the word in connection with a woman in her sixties whose son had become a schizophrenic, whose husband, in his later years, had become severely depressed, whose four children never seemed able to get together because she was so busy with her psychological manipulations of them. It was a sad story, and in the conventional psychiatric manner there was talk of the schizophrenogenic mother, the guilt this somewhat witchy person must have felt unconsciously as she played off her daughters, one against the other, and as she saw the life of her son, who never really recovered, gradually unfold in all its restricted confusion. Her defense against recognizing the ongoing troubles of those others, and of herself, was to play the armchair psychologist. When she wasn't playing the recorder or going from one lunch to another (and sneaking drinks), she was peddling psychological interpretations to anyone willing to listen.

A dreary case history, one of many Miss Freud had heard during the course of her long clinical life. She made some shrewd and knowing comments about the mother's brittle nature, supposedly masked by her pseudopsychology, which was meant to show a "with-it" personality, and she was in the middle of further comments on psychodynamics when she interrupted herself, and said,

"Here is someone who is spending the last years of her life playing psychological games with herself and all the people around her. What are we to do? How are we to get through all those layers of evasion and illusion? She is not about to go through a psychoanalysis and see how angry she is and understand the reasons for her meanness or her tricky talk. I'm not even sure she ever could have been analyzed: we would probably say she's not strong enough psychologically to take the kind of awareness our patients struggle for. I think, frankly, what she really aches to have is *forgiveness*. She is pursued by her own furies. She needs a rest from the demons that have been un-leashed by her own mind on others and have haunted her, as well – through those others: the damage they've sustained. If she were a bit more religious, if she could get down on her knees and pray, perhaps she would obtain relief. But I doubt she will find that solace. She needs forgiveness – to forgive her-self, to be forgiven. In our field, forgiveness is an unknown idea."

Anna Freud was not about to embrace religion, yet she realized that at a certain point psychoanalytic interpretation was not what some people require, or can find helpful. I kept thinking of that conversation with Anna Freud as I heard Dorothy Day talk about forgiveness – the convergence of themes in two elderly women of such different sensibilities.[14] There was a wry reflectiveness in Dorothy Day which connected her to Anna Freud; both had a healthy respect for this life's continuing ironies and ambiguities. Anna Freud was an avid reader of Tolstoy and Dostoievski, a side of her Dorothy Day would have keenly appreciated. Moreover, when Dorothy Day wanted to be "psychological" she managed rather well, often using a storyteller such as Dickens to make her point about the human mind.

"A long time ago I read *Bleak House* and I'll never forget the phrase Dickens used about one of the characters, her 'telescopic philanthropy.' I forget the name of the person, but she was someone who neglected her own family while being preoccu-pied with the problems of distant natives in Africa or Asia or wherever. For a while the two words kept ringing in my ears: an accusation. I was in the middle of my Greenwich Village life, full of concerns for people everywhere, but not doing the best job with my personal life. I would get angry with myself for letting those words bother me. I said to myself: *Someone* has to stand up for people far away from us who are being exploited or who are starving to death. What's *wrong* with telescopic philanthropy? I would ask the question, and I would mobilize my answers to it, but I was *still* upset. I felt – inside me, some-place – that Dickens had someone like me in mind when he wrote those words. I remember, once, feeling torn between the desire to throw that book [*Bleak House*] out the window, and a desire to brand myself with the initials T.P., my 'scarlet letters.'

"I'm being foolish now – I was being foolish then: melo-dramatic. But seriously, we have our risks to run, all of us, and I think Dickens had taken the measure of many of us when he gave us telescopic philanthropy. One of our rowdier men got surly with me once as he sat and stared at the soup we had made for him and his friends. I think he picked up some terrible streak in me: I kept staring at the soup and wondering why he wasn't taking any and thinking of all the work that goes into getting the vegetables and preparing them, and also thinking that [the soup] was getting colder and colder. And suddenly he turned on me and said he wished I would mind my own busi-ness and not mind his, and why didn't I just go and have the soup myself, and stop trying to feel good by pushing it on him. Oh, I was upset with him. I told him no one had to come and have soup or coffee or anything – we're not rounding people up. But I did go on a bit, and the longer my explanation lasted, the more uncomfortable I became with myself. That phrase 'telescopic philanthropy' came to my mind, and I was ready to pour the soup down the drain, or on that man's head! He never did touch a drop of it, nor did I, that day. I think I was ready to banish Mr. Charles Dickens from my bookshelf."

The theme of forgiveness in Dickens was important to Dorothy Day; she returned to it constantly. As might be expected, she also recognized the religious side, his Christian imagery in *Little Dorrit*, and, of course, the dramatic moment at the end of *A Tale of Two*

Cities when Sydney Carton willingly goes to the guillotine with these words on his lips, "I am the Resurrection and the Life, saith the Lord: he that believeth in me shall never die!" Though she could readily find those words in her Bible, she sometimes chose to find them in the last page or so of *A Tale of Two Cities*.

She also loved Orwell's famous essay on Dickens, especially the excerpt in it from a letter he wrote to his youngest son in 1868. She had copied the lines down on a piece of paper and mentioned it to me several times. Once she read it aloud.

You will remember that you have never at home been harassed about religious observance, or mere formalities. I have always been anxious not to weary my children with such things, before they are old enough to form opinions respecting them. You will therefore understand the better that I now most solemnly impress upon you the truth and beauty of the Christian Religion, as it came from Christ Himself, and the impossibility of your going far wrong if you humbly but heartily respect it . . . Never abandon the wholesome practice of saying your own private prayers, night and morning. I have never abandoned it myself, and I know the comfort of it.

There was in Dorothy Day a distinct Protestant side that resisted all her years of Catholic loyalty. She emphasized the phrase "as it came from Christ Himself" as she read, and she made clear, afterward, how much those words meant to her. She had told me often how much she enjoyed her private moments or her personal moments with Him – away from church. She also admitted, occasionally, her rebellious times as a Catholic, when the complex dealings of the hierarchy ("all the intrigue in those layers and layers of officeholders") would get to her.

But despite her Protestant, anarchist side she loved the rituals and ceremonies, even the institutional authority, of the Catholic church. She loved being able to disappear, she once put it, into a particular neighborhood church, sit alone, pray and meditate, and find herself yet again. She recognized the continuity all these churches offered her in the course of her travels across the country.

Like the books, they were utter essentials. She even carried some of her books into church.

"I don't think our Lord minds if we see Him in books other than His book. I remember some of my trips – the best moments: being in a city where I don't know many people, and I have just got there, at the bus terminal. I have been reading a story of Tolstoy or Chekhov, or I took *Bread and Wine* with me, again, and I find a Catholic church near the bus station, or I walk and walk and finally there's one, and I just go inside and sit and try to settle a few things going on in my life. I'll pray or confess directly to God, and I'll even tell Him what I've been reading. I've often wondered whether some of these books which seem to be so inspired, even exalted in their wisdom – whether our Lord hasn't had a close, direct hand in their creation. Oh, I know, the Lord created *everything*, but I'm talking about a special intervention."

No sooner had she said that than she was ready to turn on the remark.

"There is so much beauty in this world. Why do I single out books? I just saw a mother with a baby on the bus: as much beauty and grace there as in any book. The way she held the child, spoke to the child, the way the child looked at her and beamed at her – God's love was there, as it is in *Bread and Wine* or in Alyosha's personality, or in Sonia at the end of *Crime and Punishment*, or in the long-suffering little Dorrit. So many of us who write are trying to go beyond writing, to those silent moments between a mother and a baby. But, of course, we don't quite get there, as writers, at least. Sometimes I find myself in a strange church in a strange part of a strange city, and I feel God nearer than ever, as if He becomes our anchor most firmly when we're least connected with the daily anchors of our lives. I think writers like Silone or Dostoievski were trying to break out of their lives, even their writing lives, and find . . . God, the meaning of things, a purpose, faith: all those words we use — and they sound so banal, I know, but in the heat of searching the words take on life."

She was always trying to be alone with God, yet she lived in a community where it was hard to find even the conventional privacy of the comfortable bourgeois life. She was always trying to get her own particular moment with God, with Jesus, yet she also loved the crowds in certain Catholic churches and the submergence of all those individuals in worship. She craved secluded study, to be lost in thought and prayer — the nearer the ocean the better — yet she lived near urban din and engaged daily in dozens of collective projects. Though she had both a contemplative and prophetic mind, her life was an active, essentially pastoral one: feed the hungry, house the needy, care for the sick. She was an earthy, political, practical-minded person, yet she could be almost willfully blind to the world's habits and priorities as she persisted in the direction of her faith.

Many times, as I tried to understand some of these contradictions and after trying to find an answer in her writings, I would give up and take the matter to her directly. Once I asked her how she would want to be described if someone asked about her and about her life. We laughed about the risks of autobiography and biography, the elusiveness of each and every life, the particularity that defies the abstractions. She first made sure that I remembered her pleasure in appreciating this life's contradictions and its inevitable inconsistencies, as if I had much chance of forgetting while contemplating her life. She then took up the challenge and repeated what I had heard before — her wish to be defined and remembered as a member of a particular Christian community, as an ardent seeker after God who, with some devotion, had followed His example "after a few false starts." Then, after pausing to look out the window, after a retreat into silence, she said slowly, quoting the archbishop of Paris, Cardinal Suhard,[15] "To be a witness does not consist in engaging in propaganda or even in stirring people up, but in being a living mystery; it means to live in such a way that one's life would not make sense if God did not exist."

Notes

Preface

1. Each year, for a while, the students in my freshman seminar at Harvard College went to one or more of those houses. In the seminar we examined the "literary-documentary tradition," using, especially, James Agee's *Let Us Now Praise Famous Men* and George Orwell's *Down and Out in London and Paris*, *The Road to Wigan Pier*, and *Homage to Catalonia*. A central and continuing matter for discussion in the seminar was the difficulty of leaving one world in order to be part of another and the related question of how others, different in certain ways, regard a so-called outsider, whether an observer or so-called activist, or indeed both. For several years Dorothy Day and others in the Catholic Worker community of Boston and New York were exceedingly gracious and generous with their time and advice. One memorable Friday she talked with us at great length and from the heart, telling us of her doubts as well as her strong sense of responsibility. "Sometimes I don't know what we're doing here — whether we should be here at all," she remarked to one of the students in the course of an intense conversation. "Then I'll see a friendly look on the face of someone who only a moment earlier has been in a real bad state, and I'm grateful. The person may be poor, may be alcoholic, may have no place to spend the night, but she's been able — or he — to

help us here find some direction and use for ourselves." I have used such comments in my larger undergraduate courses, "The Literature of Social Reflection" and "The Literature of Christian Reflection," in which Dorothy Day's writing figures.

2. New York: Viking Press, 1973. Dorothy Day and her friends allowed the photographer Jon Erikson generous access to the daily routine of their working life.

3. Reading, Mass.: Addison-Wesley, 1987.

4. See Selected Bibliography, pages 172–173. The reader may be interested in this comment made by Dorothy Day in 1971, when I suggested to her that her life's story should be written: "In a world I won't see, but I wish I would, the biographies of some others here, including a few whom we serve lunch to, would be written, and they'd be read as eagerly as you say one of me would be read." I detected no false modesty in her manner as she spoke those words. She was passionate, even upset, and aware that in our society, with its cult of transient celebrity, attention can be a prelude to dismissal.

5. Over fifty hours of taped discussions in seventeen meetings and many others in which I took notes. Notes of my earlier talks with her go back to the 1950s.

Chapter 1
A Life Remembered

1. William Miller gives one chapter the title "Adrift." Dorothy Day used that word about herself, and not only in connection with her youth. Once she characterized her mind as "inclined to be drifting in nature," hence the great importance, she added, of "the gift of faith": a means by which she could find "direction rather than drift."

2. Several times she remarked on how the sight of the ocean helped her write, and once, somewhat facetiously, she asked me for a psychoanalytic explanation. As I paused, took a deep breath, and readied myself for a speech on the futility of such explanations,

she abruptly shifted the conversation to Dickens's novels, which we'd been discussing earlier.

3. She was, at times, wry and relaxed in that self-scrutiny; at other times she could be quite critical of herself, perhaps more so than many of us who admonish one another not to go on "guilt trips," not to be "too hard" on ourselves, would find congenial.

4. A repeated worry; I count fifteen separate occasions when it came up in the course of our talks.

5. Another concern constantly mentioned; she uttered that quotation many times.

6. Dorothy Day's presence meant a lot to many of the students I knew in SNCC (the Student Non-Violent Coordinating Committee). Several of them, who mentioned her often, came from homes in which she had been a moral presence for a long time.

7. In early December 1979.

Chapter 2
An Inquiring Idealism

1. I have even wondered whether the professedly Catholic members of certain hospitality houses have not sometimes been in a distinct minority.

2. See the discussion of Maurin in *A Spectacle Unto the World*, and in Marc Ellis, *Peter Maurin: Prophet in the Twentieth Century* (New York: Paulist Press, 1981).

3. On other occasions she was clearly uninterested in such discussions.

4. Anna Freud was similarly impressed with "curiosity" as an element of idealism, though she had a different notion about the source of that curiosity: psychological energy at work, rather than the more cognitive emphasis in this statement of Dorothy Day's.

5. Miss Freud had read that letter in *The Long Loneliness*, found it "stirring" and at times "worrying." Once she commented, "She

is, by her own description, still very much lonely. I wonder whether she is being as philosophical or existential when she uses that word, as you seem to think."

6. See volume 1 of *Children of Crisis* (Boston: Atlantic/Little, Brown, 1967).

7. My wife and I heard similar remarks in the course of our interviews for *Women of Crisis*, volumes 1 and 2 (New York: Delacorte Press, 1978, 1980).

8. In answering these questions, Dorothy Day displayed a point of view resembling George Eliot's sensibility in the preface to *Middlemarch* and in its final chapters. Eliot allows for chance and circumstance, for luck, good and bad, and for accidents and unpredictable incidents, not to mention grace: a contrast with the psychological or socioeconomic determinisms which figure so prominently in our contemporary culture.

9. It lasted four hours, during which I must have drunk ten cups of tea, which Day constantly kept offering me.

10. She referred often to Silone's evocation of that hunger in *Bread and Wine*.

11. She had a vivid memory of Chicago's street life and could still remember, also, the locations of various stores, movie houses, and churches.

12. She had a similar intensity of recall for New Orleans and could visualize and render in colorful description certain streets and neighborhoods.

13. In her seventies, she could still be sardonic with respect to even religious jargon.

14. A tough kind of self-confrontation, she once called such a discussion.

15. When I asked Day who that friend was, she smiled and said she wasn't going to "indict someone else," only herself.

16. I was unnecessarily hesitant in my delivery; worship of Dorothy Day is not what she wanted or deserved.

17. See volumes 1 and 2 of *Children of Crisis* (Boston: Atlantic/Little Brown, 1967, 1972).

18. Only a little. She turned to novels rather than Freudian theory as a background for introspection.

Chapter 3
Conversion

1. "Systematic Theology," in the spring of 1956 at Harvard.

2. Part 2 of *The Long Loneliness*, which Dorothy Day titled "Natural Happiness."

3. At other times she declared that she had "consciously prayed" long before that occasion, sometimes even "a whole lot," but not as persistently or consistently, one gathers.

4. Pascal's introspection in the *Pensées*, however, was thoroughly shrewd in its psychology.

5. My wife had encouraged me to ask these questions: "You may not be giving her enough credit. Don't you think she's had to contend with those kinds of questions? She lived in Greenwich Village and had many radical friends and must have had questions like those thrown at her for years; she must have asked them of herself."

6. She loved this well-known line in that book: "I would rather feel compunction of heart for my sins than merely know the definition of compunction."

7. Like Walker Percy and others, Day was much interested in Guardini's ideas and read and reread portions of *The End of the Modern World*.

Chapter 4
The Church Obeyed and Challenged

1. Such as Dwight MacDonald, who did a Profile of Dorothy Day for *The New Yorker*; W. H. Auden, who visited her on the Lower East Side; and Hannah Arendt, who sent her husband's clothes to St. Joseph's House upon his death.

2. Bernanos had a strong populist side to his royalist conservatism. In *The Diary of a Country Priest* he makes devastating

comments (through the curé's journal entries) about the hypocrisies and pretense the church continues to harbor. Dorothy Day loved that book, especially for its candid evocation of the best and the worst in the church's everyday life.

3. Flannery O'Connor was also much interested in Hawthorne's daughter Rose and mentions her in her collection of literary essays *Mystery and Manners* (New York: Farrar, Straus and Giroux, 1962).

4. Maurin was constantly working over the Tawney theme – the manner in which the Christian religion (Catholicism, too) had become connected to capitalist ideology and vice versa: a merging of ideologies in the daily lives of many people.

5. So often in the American South and elsewhere religion has exerted quite the contrary effect – as a constraining force on the populism of rural people who are down on their luck and have every reason to wonder why.

6. Dorothy Day saw, early on, the reactionary nature of Stalinism, and its murderous side; she also saw that Franco was a Fascist who cared little for the poor. Although she could not stomach the virulent anticlericalism of the Loyalist side, she remained devoted to the cause of the Spanish unions, the working people of the country.

7. On a later occasion, when I asked her point-blank whether she would have closed down *The Catholic Worker* if the cardinal had ordered her to do so, she replied, "Oh, I don't think he'd have ever let himself get into that kind of situation." She would go no further, but she had a broad smile on her face.

Chapter 5
A Localist Politics

1. A number of young people have brought to their Catholic Worker experience a liberal or socialist perspective which emphasizes the role of government in achieving reform.

2. In an undergraduate course I taught in 1978–1979, "Moral and Social Inquiry."

3. Dorothy Day was, even in her last years, a journalist at heart, able to read between the lines and connect a story to other events taking place. She read the *New York Times* with a keen sense of history and with memories of years of political struggles in which she had been a participant.

4. Not the word *libertarian* as it is used by some today, however – demanding liberty that is in no way balanced by a concern for the needs and difficulties of others.

5. She had read Emmanuel Mounier's writings and was well acquainted with *Esprit*, the "personalism" that emerged as a persuasive philosophical and political movement in France after the Second World War. The movement emphasized the individual, rather than the state, as the agent of reform – a reform from within and then outward, a kind of egalitarian existentialism connected to social and political activity and with a strong moral element. Such a movement, obviously, was a response to the totalitarianism of both right and left, the state-centered ideologies, which had dominated Europe for so long.

6. Dorothy Day had never been as taken with Roosevelt as some of her friends on the moderate left were during the 1930s, though she knew how much worse things might have been for the poor in the country without him.

7. Discussions with Day, in this regard, were quite taxing, and she would often tell me that it was a subject she used to hate getting into, though, of course, she felt she had to do so, again and again.

8. I have heard her read particular passages from that part of the novel with great emotion in her voice.

9. Her copy of the book was well used. She remembered various editions of it.

10. Dorothy Day had read much of what Simone Weil wrote and regarded her highly, though at times her enthusiasm was tempered by impatience or misgivings. Once she commented on Weil this way: "I haven't read her as closely as I should because she's too cerebral, at times, for me." On another occasion she observed that "perhaps she was too preoccupied, too much the victim of

her brilliant mind's tyranny. . . . I know I couldn't keep up with her if I met her for a talk." She was not inclined to discuss Weil's ideas in detail as I often wished she would.

11. A number of Weil's readers have compared her to Edmund Burke, calling his phrase a "partnership between those who are living, those who are dead and those who are to be born," an apt description of her mystical views of patriotism. She saw that the soil, the place where one's life is lived, can be the source of one's rootedness *if* the nation in question encourages that kind of patriotism.

Chapter 6
Living in a House of Hospitality

1. Dorothy Day and her coworkers always stressed this point. It is a hard one for those of us who are brought up to regard ourselves highly to keep in mind and comprehend in all its significance.

2. She was constantly afraid of the temptation to self-righteousness. "If we end up pointing our fingers at others, we demean ourselves and what we're trying to do."

3. Many who volunteer in hospitality houses observe that the intensity of pain and need in others can overwhelm a person attempting to be of assistance.

4. It was never far from her; even when she was traveling it went along.

5. It is called *Trabajador Católicó de Houston*. The hospitality house is called Casa Juan Diego.

6. She loved *Middlemarch*, had read it "several times," and quoted from it often.

7. I have tried to understand and document the nature of this ironic problem in *The Mind's Fate* (Boston: Little, Brown, 1975) and volume 5 of *Children of Crisis: Privileged Ones: The Well-Off and the Rich in America* (Boston: Little, Brown, 1978). Once I heard Dorothy Day summarize her view of such a paradox with a biblical phrase: "Jesus told us that the last shall be first, and the

first last, and he may have had what you've been mentioning in mind, along with lots of other ironies, as you call them."

Chapter 7
Her Spiritual Kin

1. Once, on an especially grim afternoon, when some fairly troubled guests, full of noise and threats and small-scale but unnerving truculence had been served lunch by Dorothy Day, she retired for a few moments and read from a book of poems of Saint John of the Cross. When she came back to the kitchen area she was smiling again, a cheerful presence among the others who were still trying to shake off a few tense encounters.

2. She especially loved *David Copperfield, Great Expectations,* and *Little Dorrit.*

3. She had read all his novels more than once, I believe. She was always mentioning *The Brothers Karamazov* and *Crime and Punishment.*

4. She'd read Tolstoy's *War and Peace* and *Anna Karenina,* of course, and *Resurrection* which she much loved, and his stories and, too, his moral essays, such as *The Kingdom of God Is Within You* and *Confession,* to which she often referred. Tolstoy's personal story of a religious journey – the intellectual finding his way to a day-to-day faith – meant a lot to her, and she invariably mentioned that latter essay when the question of skepticism and doubt among the intelligentsia was being discussed.

5. Dorothy Day loved his stories and plays; she had even found *The Island,* the young doctor Chekhov's documentary account of his medical work among sick prisoners on Sakhalin Island.

6. She had spent many hours reading Maritain and many more talking with him. His support of her actions and ideas was important to her.

7. She quoted and read to me as much from the Old Testament as from the New. One of the qualities she scorned in Simone Weil was her sad ignorance of and hostility toward the Jewish religious tradition.

8. Day's politics became, finally, an expression of her religious faith. She understood the populist anger and decency that inspired "liberation theology," but she did not find its Marxist emphasis at all congenial. Moreover, the mystical aspect of her mind and heart was drawn to John of the Cross and others in that tradition.

9. In particular, Bonhoeffer's prison letters touched Day deeply.

10. It was a matter of "tone" Day once said, Orwell's "toughness throughout it all." She herself could be tough as she did her work in those hospitality houses – tell people to hush, urge them to sit down or take a walk. Sometimes she could calm people down with only her eyes, her facial expression.

11. She had read *Bread and Wine* "four or five times."

12. In explaining her bond with Silone, she said, "I feel we have suffered in the same way – the disappointment of politics and the hope that we don't forget others, no matter our disappointments, and the search for the meaning of life."

13. On the subject of Freudian psychology Dorothy Day once told me, "I *heard* about his ideas all the time when I was young, but when faced with a choice between him and a novel, I always chose a novel as a way to learn psychology."

14. Both Dorothy Day and Anna Freud were passionately devoted, in the course of a long life, to vulnerable people: to the poor and to troubled children.

15. Cardinal Emmanuel Celestin Suhard (1874–1949) was archbishop of Paris during World War II. In his pastoral letters he urged the French church to work among the poor and set up a Mission de Paris, which was a forerunner of the Worker Priest Movement.

Selected Bibliography

Dorothy Day was a first-rate writer who never hesitated to put before her readers the personal struggles she waged or her reasons for acting as she did. Her writing was substantial, and much of it is still available to the interested reader. Her first book was a novel, *The Eleventh Virgin* (New York: Boni, 1924); it is extremely hard to find anywhere, including libraries. Her next book begins a series of extended statements on the Catholic Worker life she found for herself and others: *From Union Square to Rome* (Silver Spring: Preservation of the Faith Press, 1938). The following year she published *House of Hospitality* (New York: Sheed and Ward, 1939). *The Long Loneliness* appeared in 1952 (New York: Harper and Row); *Loaves and Fishes* in 1963 (New York: Harper and Row). The last of her books in that series was *On Pilgrimage: The Sixties* (New York: Curtis, 1973). In those five books there are elements of reportage, religious introspection, moral reflection, political analysis, and autobiography. *The Long Loneliness*, especially, offers as much of Dorothy Day's life as she would ever put on the printed page. Finally, there is a biographical essay on one of her favorite saints, Thérèse de Lisieux, known as the "Little Flower," whose intense suffering and faith have been an inspiration to millions: *Thérèse* (Notre Dame: Fides Press, 1960).

As for her journalism, there are over fifty years' worth of her columns in *The Catholic Worker*, and dozens of articles written for *The Call,* for *Commonweal,* for *Masses,* for *Liberator,* for *New Masses,* and for the New Orleans *Item.* She was an untiring journalist, a muckraker and book reviewer and social observer become social essayist. She was also, as some of us had the good fortune to experience, a determined correspondent. Her letters were an important mode of introspection, a means of sharing herself with others, and often a major instrument of her religious life.

Several friends and admirers of Dorothy Day have studied her published work and provided us with helpful and instructive anthologies of her writing. The most recent, most erudite, and most satisfying is Robert Ellsberg's *By Little and By Little* (New York: Knopf, 1985), which contains a touching and edifying introduction to her life and work and a wonderfully trenchant analysis of its significance to so many people. *The Dorothy Day Book,* by Margaret Quigley and Michael Garvey (Springfield, Ill.: Templegate, 1982) provides glimpses of her writing and of some of her favorite "readings" – passages from books that meant a great deal to her. There is, too, Stanley Vishnewski's *Meditations: Dorothy Day* (New York: Paulist Press, 1970), a simply presented but affecting series of excerpts from her writing arranged by an old Catholic Worker colleague.

One major biography has been written: *Dorothy Day,* by William D. Miller (New York: Harper, 1982). Professor Miller taught history at Marquette University. All of us are indebted to him for his extraordinary efforts on behalf of both the Catholic Worker Movement and Dorothy Day, a dedicated and discerning intelligence that have given us not only the biography, but an earlier, comprehensive account of the entire tradition, *A Harsh and Dreadful Love: Dorothy Day and the Catholic Worker Movement* (New York: Liveright, 1973). As Professor Miller reminds us, a considerable amount of Catholic Worker "materials," including much of Dorothy Day's papers, have been placed in the Marquette University Archives, and "a statement of materials available for research" can be obtained. Moreover, those same archives contain Father Alex Avitabile's complete bibliographical list of all Dorothy Day's writings.

Worthy of special mention is *A Penny a Copy: Readings from the Catholic Worker*, edited by Thomas C. Cornell and James H. Forest (New York: MacMillan, 1968). The collection of essays is not limited to those of Dorothy Day, though some of her strongest pieces are included. One finds in her company a number of other writers who have belonged to the Catholic Worker family. I wish, here, to mention Jim Forest's great help to me when, in the early 1970s, I began to study Dorothy Day's life and the Catholic Workers' significance in both the secular and religious worlds of the twentieth century. He helped me with an earlier book, *A Spectacle Unto the World: The Catholic Worker Movement* (New York: Viking, 1973), and I would like to commend the book, unashamedly, for its photographs, taken by my friend Jon Erikson. Dorothy Day and her colleagues were not ones to welcome pho- tographers, for understandable and important reasons: the constant risk that privacy and dignity might be put in jeopardy. Jon talked at great length with the people at St. Joseph's House, as did I; eventually he stayed there, worked there, became part of the everyday scene, and so was given permission to use his camera, which I believe he did with thoughtfulness and sensitivity.

Two historians have tried to comprehend the Catholic Worker Movement and Dorothy Day's role in it with diligence and empathy. Their books supply facts and context in abundance and very helpful bibliographies: Mel Piehl, *Breaking Bread: The Catholic Worker and the Origins of Catholic Radicalism in America* (Philadelphia: Temple University, 1982), and Nancy L. Roberts, *Dorothy Day and the Catholic Worker* (Albany: State University of New York Press, 1984). The bibliography in Professor Piehl's book is especially useful, containing references to a great many articles, as well as books, which shed light on the movement and its founders. Speaking of those founders, one must mention with gratitude Marc Ellis's book, which reminds us of what Dorothy Day never stopped telling everyone she met, that Peter Maurin was an important inspiration and driving force for that movement's birth: *Peter Maurin: Prophet in the Twentieth Century* (New York: Paulist Press, 1981). Ellis's *A year at the Catholic Worker* (New York: Paulist Press, 1979) is also well worth reading.

Century (New York: Paulist Press, 1981). Ellis's *A Year at the Catholic Worker* (New York: Paulist Press, 1979) is also well worth reading.

Once when we were sitting and talking I asked Dorothy Day what she would recommend I read, if I wanted to know her better, to understand her values and principles. Her response at that moment, immediate and firm, with a wry smile on her face, strikes me as a fitting way to end this bibliographical note: "I would suggest that you read the books I have loved and kept reading over and over: Dostoievski's *Crime and Punishment* and his *Brothers Karamazov* and his *Possessed*, and Tolstoy's *Anna Karenina* and *War and Peace* and *Resurrection* and his stories, and Dickens (*David Copperfield* and *Little Dorrit*) and Bernanos, his *Diary of a Country Priest*, and Graham Greene and Mauriac and Silone – how I treasure *Bread and Wine* and go back to it at times. Well, that is a beginning for all of us!"

About the Author

Robert Coles, M.D., is professor of psychiatry and medical humanities at Harvard Medical School and research psychiatrist for the Harvard University Health Services. Among his many books are the five-volume *Children of Crisis* series, for which he was awarded the Pulitzer Prize, and works on Erik Erikson, William Carlos Williams, Walker Percy, and Flannery O'Connor. With his wife, Jane Hallowell Coles, he wrote the two volumes of *Women of Crisis*, also in the Radcliffe Biography Series. A recipient of a MacArthur Fellowship, he is continuing the research he wrote about in the much acclaimed works *The Moral Life of Children* and *The Political Life of Children*. Dr. Coles lives near Boston with his wife and three sons.

Index